D0849733

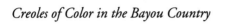

Creoles of Color in the Bayou Country

Creoles of Color
in the
Bayou Country

Carl A. Brasseaux, Keith P. Fontenot,
and Claude F. Oubre

Foreword by Clifton Carmon

UNIVERSITY PRESS OF MISSISSIPPI   JACKSON

Mitchell Memorial Library
Mississippi State University

Copyright © 1994 by the University Press of Mississippi
All rights reserved
Manufactured in the United States of America

97   96   95   94   4   3   2   1

The paper in this book meets the guidelines for permanence and durability of
the Committee on Production Guidelines for Book Longevity of the
Council on Library Resources.

Library of Congress Cataloging-in-Publication Data

Brasseaux, Carl A.
    Creoles of color in the Bayou country / Carl A. Brasseaux, Keith P.
Fontenot, and Claude F. Oubre ; foreword by Clifton Carmon.
        p.   cm.
    Includes bibliographical references (p. 155) and index.
    ISBN 0-87805-714-5 (acid-free paper)
        1. Creoles—Louisiana—History.   2. Creoles—Louisiana—Genealogy.
I. Fontenot, Keith P.   II. Oubre, Claude F., 1936–   III. Title.
F380.C87B73   1994
976.3′00444—dc20   94-20383
                                                                CIP

British Library Cataloging-in-Publication data available

Contents

ILLUSTRATIONS

FOREWORD

The history of the Creoles of Color in the prairie regions of Louisiana dates back to the early settlement of the area. Their story is deeply intertwined with the story of the growth and development of an important farming and cattle-raising area of Louisiana.

Creoles of Color in the Bayou Country is the first serious attempt to look at the history of the Creoles of Color in these regions. The authors have chronicled well a sometimes troubled but always fascinating history of a proud and calculating people. They have delved extensively into primary records and have found a people intricately involved in the economic activities of the area.

From the earliest days of settlement and establishment in the prairie regions, the Creoles of Color, it seems, were in the business of seeking prosperity. In this endeavor, certainly, they received a greater degree of help than other free blacks. They were then, as so many are today, concerned about what others in society thought of them. Consequently, they were a people driven constantly to succeed, a value that was not lost on their progeny. In a three-tier society—white, free people of color, and slaves—many struggled, but they demonstrated much persistence in their attempt to be an integral part of the community.

The Creoles of Color were good imitators. They were not interested in being black. They were truly a people apart—they did not belong and were not accepted as members of the white race nor were they willing to be members of the Negro race. If they could not be accepted into the white race, then they would attempt to be as white as they could. By a few years before the Civil War many had developed an elitist attitude regarding their social relationships. They imitated the life-style of their white neighbors. They were members of the Catholic church, spoke the French language, and in the antebellum years owned Negro slaves. Slave ownership by this group was not necessarily a benevolent undertaking but rather an economic enterprise.

With the end of the Civil War, the Creoles of Color had to confront the definition of their role and place in the community and in society. The three-tier status they had experienced during the antebellum years no longer existed. Almost overnight they were thrust into a group many considered their inferiors. In her recent book, *The Sweeter the Juice: A Family Memoir in Black and White,* Shirlee Taylor Haizlip concludes that it was common for light-skinned blacks to pass for white. Certainly some of the Creoles of Color not only passed but in fact *became* white. Doing so frequently required them to forsake members of their families. The larger question—one that is perhaps not fully answered even to-day—is one of motivation. Certainly racism with its concomitant pro-scriptions of opportunities for blacks to advance in society played a role. The question, however, whether there were other reasons still remains.

Some Creoles of Color had for many years played a significant role in the economic affairs of their respective communities. After the Civil War they were denied a separate status in these communities. To main-tain some semblance of status in a community increasing in population, some of them found it necessary to relocate to have sufficient agricul-tural land. The enclaves they developed served two purposes for them: they had the land they sought for agricultural purposes, and these en-claves isolated them, allowing them to be with their own and to main-tain their distinctive way of life. They became clannish, moving apart from society more than they had ever done before. They nevertheless continued to cherish wholesome family life and to maintain a deep re-spect for hard work, their religion, and their property.

Clifton Carmon
Opelousas, Louisiana

Few words in American English are as misunderstood or as frequently misused as the term *Creole*. Because of the myriad misconceptions surrounding the word, it is necessary to define the term as it is presently used by students of Louisiana history and culture. For the linguist, *creole* (lowercase "c") can signify either the hybrid language formed of French and West African linguistic elements or the individuals who speak the idiom. Creole-speakers, of course, can—and do—come from varied ethnic and racial backgrounds. The picture is further complicated because many individuals—both black and white—who identify themselves as Creole speak Cajun French instead of creole. This is particularly true in the prairie region of southwestern Louisiana, where Cajun French has traditionally functioned as the lingua franca. Unlike Creole Cajun-French-speakers, who generally trace their ancestry to antebellum free persons of color, black and white creole-speakers are usually descendants respectively of slaves or slave owners who learned the language from their black domestics. Many, if not most, creole-speakers can point to ancestors who fled Saint Domingue's black revolution in the late 1790s and early 1800s.

The historian interprets the term quite differently, based on the common usage of the word in historical documents. For eighteenth-century Louisianians, "Creole" (uppercase "c") signified "of local origin." Hence black and white children born in the colony were designated Creole to distinguish them from Louisiana's European and African settlers. In the early eighteenth century, white Creoles were considered to be socially inferior to immigrants from the Continent, although once established as an economic force within the colony, white Creoles came to consider themselves a social aristocracy within Louisiana (Brasseaux, 1987:

167–76). Native-born blacks were generally regarded as more valuable than imported slaves because they were already acclimated and theoretically spoke French. There were also Creole varieties of vegetables and livestock (Oukada 1979; Tregle 193–98).

The term was indelibly imprinted upon the white Creole community by an almost uninterrupted influx of continental French, Canadian, Caribbean, and, later, pan-European French-speakers and the resulting need to distinguish native from immigrant Frenchmen. The "Creole" designation for native-born blacks fell from common usage after the Louisiana Purchase (1803) because shortly after the acquisition of the French colony from France, Congress banned the importation of slaves into Louisiana. The colonial usage of the term was revived after the Civil War, when former free blacks sought to distinguish themselves from freedmen (emancipated slaves). Recoiling in horror from the renewed usage of the term by African-Americans and the resulting confusion over the racial identity it created, white Creoles throughout Louisiana gradually abandoned their traditional ethnic identity, thereby eventually creating the false impression among outsiders that Creoles were exclusively either blacks or people of mixed racial parentage (a misconception perpetuated by popular writers of the late twentieth century) (Brasseaux and Allain).

Other historical terms may prove equally confusing to the uninitiated. The word *mulatto* is used throughout this narrative in the same sense in which it was commonly used in the nineteenth century—as a generic designation for all persons of mixed racial (i.e., Caucasian and Negroid) background. *Mulatto* consequently denoted a wide range of phenotypes, but in the southwestern Louisiana context, it generally indicated persons of *café au lait,* or lighter, skin color. In early southwestern Louisiana, mulattoes constituted an overwhelming majority of the free persons of color—blacks manumitted during the era of slavery— who were the progenitors of the region's Creole of Color community.

These free people of color, most of whom were Francophones, frequently identified themselves in civil records with the French term *gens de couleur libre* (free persons of color). Enjoying most of the legal rights of whites as well as a higher legal and social status than the enslaved population, free men and women of color jealously guarded their privileged position in antebellum African-American society. Indeed, the civil records indicate that they continued to identify themselves as *gens de couleur libre* to distinguish themselves from former slaves long after the Emancipation Proclamation had destroyed the legal basis for such a distinction.

This desire to preserve their social position and cultural identity led directly to the creation of the Creole of Color community in the prairie parishes. Historians have only recently begun to assess the contributions of the latter-day Creoles—the Creoles of Color—to rural Louisiana's early development (Sterkx; Mills; Baker and Kreamer). This book is the first serious attempt to chronicle and interpret the long and proud history of the previously overlooked Creoles of Color of the prairie parishes.

Charting the course of the prairie community's early development is a challenging undertaking, for traditional primary sources are virtually nonexistent. Little personal correspondence has survived, and news accounts, generally limited to diatribes by white supremacist journalists, provide little illumination. In addition, many ecclesiastical records have been closed to public scrutiny by Catholic officials concerned about potential leaks of "sensitive" information regarding miscegenation among Louisiana's prominent and influential first families.

The civil records of Louisiana's parish courthouses, however, provide a wealth of information regarding the economic development of the black Creole community. Conveyance, mortgage, and donation records not only contain bequests by white property owners to their common-law wives and natural children, thereby illuminating the often murky origins of many Creole of Color families, but also permit researchers to plot the acquisition of wealth by families over generations. Successions (probates) record the orderly transfer of property between generations and provide the best available guide to material culture in early black Creole households.

Registers of civil suits lend insight into the effective use of the local legal system by Creoles of Color. These resources indicate, for the first time, not only that prairie Creoles of Color were well aware of their legal rights but that they were very aggressive in using the legal system to protect their property and civil rights.

The wealth of economic data in the civil archives is complemented by myriad federal census schedules. Free people of color are clearly delineated in federal censuses of the early and mid-nineteenth century. The surnames adopted by the *gens de couleur libre* during this period serve as accurate guideposts to data on Creoles of Color in the postbellum lists. Antebellum and postbellum census reports collectively provide considerable insight into the economic status of the Creole of Color community vis-à-vis neighboring racial and ethnic groups. In addition, the census reports, though admittedly flawed by inept record-keeping and, in 1870, popular resistance to the head count, provide the best hard data regarding black Creole demographics, slaveholdings, agricultural activities, and occupational pursuits. These data are both particularly rich and particularly valuable.

The two-dimensional images of black Creole society found in the federal census reports are given depth by eyewitness accounts of Creole of Color responses to successive local crises immediately before, during, and after the Civil War. Alexandre Barde's "official" history of the 1859 vigilante movement chronicles the rapid deterioration of race relations in the prairie country. The persistence of local factional violence during and after the Civil War is recorded in the *Official Records of the War of the Rebellion* and the reports of congressional investigative committees.

Taken together, all of the foregoing documentary resources provide a fairly complete view of a highly insular society whose written and oral traditions remain largely inaccessible to non-Creole researchers. Justifiably proud of their ancestors' notable achievements, many modern Creoles of Color are also equally ashamed of their forefathers' slaveholdings and elitism—hence their great reluctance either to discuss the early history of the community with outsiders or to grant them access to historical documents and memorabilia.

The authors have explored as many facets of the obscure and insular culture as the documentary record permits. This record shows the prairie Creoles of Color to have been a diverse people: planters, farmers, shopkeepers, ranchers, land speculators, and entrepreneurs. These varied elements of black Creole society were bound tightly together by racial, cultural, linguistic, religious, and social homogeneity. These shared attributes, coupled with a strong work ethic and a distinctive place in the region's multitiered society, created the perception, both within the Creole of Color community and among neighboring ethnic and racial groups, that the prairie country's mixed-racial denizens were truly a people apart.

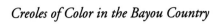

Creoles of Color in the Bayou Country

CHAPTER ONE

Origins and Early Development

Unwilling or unable to grapple with the complexity of south Louisiana's polyglot population, many popular writers either restrict the scope of their work to only one segment of the society—usually focusing on the Cajuns, who are often perceived by outsiders as the region's most "exotic" people—or attempt to simplify the problem of ethnic and racial diversity by dealing in broad, often inaccurate generalizations. For example, many writers portray the region's white and black communities as monolithic groups, ignoring the class and cultural cleavages that have traditionally fragmented them. Creoles of Color are consequently often lost in the shuffle, despite their demographic importance and significant contributions to the region's development (Griffin 147–52; Dismukes 7–48).

Creoles of Color are among the "first families" of southwestern Louisiana. Most Creole of Color families trace their ancestry to African slaves imported from present-day Mali, Senegal, and, to a lesser extent, from other West African nations and later manumitted for various reasons. Some slaves earned their release through military service, particularly during the Natchez War (1729–31), or for outstanding public service. Other bondsmen were emancipated as a reward for long and faithful service to their masters (Sterkx 18–19), while still other slaves who could prove any Indian ancestry were freed by Louisiana's Spanish colonial government in compliance with a ban on Indian slavery in the Spanish empire. Some New Orleans–area slaves purchased their freedom with the proceeds of jobs performed on Sundays and holidays. This practice, however, was rare on the Attakapas and Opelousas frontier. Finally, some manumitted slaves were the mistresses or natural children of white farmers (Sterkx 18–20, 26–28, 59–67).

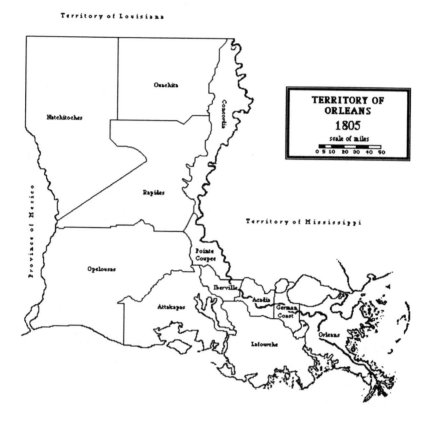

Territory of Louisiana

TERRITORY OF
ORLEANS
1805
scale of miles
0 5 10 20 30 40 50

Ouachita

Concordia

Natchitoches

Rapides

Province of Mexico

Territory of Mississippi

Pointe
Coupee

Opelousas

Iberville

Acadia

Attakapas

German
Coast

Orleans

Lafourche

As the eighteenth century progressed, however, manumissions for heroic or faithful service as well as unlawful bondage grew increasingly rare, while the release of mistresses and their mulatto children became more and more commonplace, resulting in the dramatic growth of Louisiana's free black population in the late eighteenth and early nineteenth centuries. The 1763 census of lower Louisiana, for example, lists only 82 free persons of color (FPCs), all of whom resided in the New Orleans area; the free black community, however, grew rapidly in subsequent years, rising to 1,701 in 1788; 3,350 in 1806; 16,710 in 1830; 17,462 in 1850; and 18,467 in 1860. Rapid population growth was matched by a corresponding rise in economic status (Sterkx 85, 95, 98).

The development of a free black society in southwestern Louisiana's prairie parishes offers a microcosmic view of these statewide economic

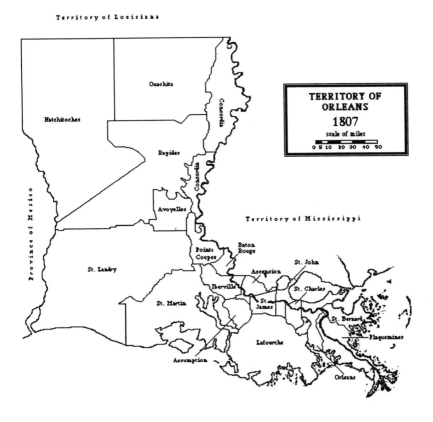

Territory of Louisiana

TERRITORY OF
ORLEANS
1807
scale of miles
0 5 10 20 30 40 50

Ouachita

Concordia

Natchitoches

Rapides

Concordia

Avoyelles

Territory of Mississippi

Province of Mexico

Pointe
Coupee

Baton
Rouge

St. John

St. Landry

Ascension

St. Charles

Iberville

St. Martin

St.
James

St. Bernard

Lafourche

Plaquemines

Assumption

Orleans

and demographic trends. The ethnogenesis and embryonic development of these rural Creole of Color communities occurred in the Attakapas and Opelousas posts, two civil and military districts that, in the
late eighteenth and early nineteenth centuries, comprised the entire
south-central and southwestern quadrants of modern-day Louisiana.
Attakapas encompassed the present parishes of Lafayette, Vermilion,
St. Martin, Iberia, and St. Mary, while Opelousas was composed of the
territory presently contained in St. Landry, Evangeline, Acadia, Jeffer-
son Davis, Allen, Cameron, Calcasieu, and Beauregard parishes. The
Attakapas and Opelousas regions retained their colonial designations
long after the districts had been subdivided into civil parishes in the
early decades of the nineteenth century. These regional designations
were not confined to local usages. The United States Census Bureau,

for example, referred to this region as Attakapas in 1810 although the area had been renamed St. Martin Parish by the state legislature three years earlier.

Because indigenous inhabitants of the lower prairies—the Attakapas Indians—were reputedly cannibalistic, the Attakapas and Opelousas districts were among the last areas of lower Louisiana to be developed by the colony's French government. Indeed, the French administration made no effort to establish formal relations with the Attakapas, the area's largest indigenous group, and the Opelousas, a cultural and linguistic subgroup of the Attakapas, throughout the first four decades of Louisiana's existence, prompting the tribe to send a delegation to New Orleans in 1733 to forge commercial ties with the neighboring colony. If traders were sent into their territory, the Indian delegates maintained, the tribes would exchange deer pelts, tallow (deer fat and bear oil), and horses smuggled from Spanish Texas for French manufactured goods.

Though he received the delegation graciously, Governor Jean-Baptiste Le Moyne de Bienville did nothing to promote commercial relations with the Attakapas, believing that the tribe's perceived backwardness, nomadic habits, apparent laziness, and reputed cannibalism would render any trading enterprise unprofitable. In the late 1730s, however, a small number of French entrepreneurs successfully ventured into the prairie country and traded blue beads, guns, and other manufactured items for deer pelts and tallow. Though small in scale, trade with the Indians remained sufficiently profitable and stable to justify the establishment of a trading post near present-day Port Barre in the late 1740s (De Ville 27–33).

Throughout the late 1740s and 1750s, a handful of French traders remained the only semipermanent European settlers in Attakapas and Opelousas territory. Not until the 1760s did colonial governors appoint commandants, thereby formally creating political subdivisions in those formerly marginal areas, and open the new districts to full-scale development. Small numbers of slaves accompanied the few French settlers—mostly adventurers and retired military personnel—who first ventured into the Attakapas and Opelousas districts with the intention of establishing ranches in those areas. These black and white pioneers were joined in subsequent years by numerous retired French enlisted men, Acadian exiles, African slaves, and *gens de couleur libre*—free blacks whose descendants now constitute the overwhelming majority of Creoles of Color in the prairie parishes (Voorhies 124–28, 280–365).

The first free black mentioned in the records of the prairie posts was one Louis, a "free mulatto"—probably from the New Orleans area—who, in 1766, resided with his wife, Josine, and daughter Nanette in the Opelousas district. According to the 1774 census of Opelousas (folios 106–10), as well as a Spanish land grant conveying to him title to property in the Baton Rouge area in 1787, "Louis" f.m.c. is identified as "Louis Ricar[d]." He had prospered during the intervening years. The 1774 census report indicates that he owned two slaves, fifty cattle, six horses or mules, and ten hogs—at a time when only 22.79 percent of all Opelousas district households possessed slaves and only 18.38 of all freeholders possessed as many as fifty cows.

Other free blacks who subsequently made their homes along the southwestern Louisiana frontier, settling in the Attakapas district, also fared well economically, thanks largely to the beneficence of their liberators. Sometime before 1774, André Masse, the largest slaveholder (in the 1766 census, he owned twenty slaves) among the Attakapas/Opelousas pioneers, emancipated six Negro families and endowed each with significant numbers of livestock (Census of Opelousas, folios 106–10). Three slave families freed around 1774 by Attakapas commandant Gabriel Fuselier de la Claire also received generous quantities of cows, horses, and pigs. To put their collective economic standing in proper perspective, median livestock holdings for the black ranchers were 9.7 cows, 3.7 horses (or mules), and 5.0 hogs—figures exceeding comparable holdings for 20 percent of all local white households (Voorhies 280–83).

Though small, the new free black communities of Attakapas and Opelousas compared favorably with the more established but equally tiny free black communities in the New Orleans area. For example, New Orleans and the nearby settlements of Chapitoulas and English Bend boasted respectively twenty, fifteen, and sixteen free black settlers. Attakapas and Opelousas had respectively fifteen and seven free black residents—a group collectively larger than its counterpart in the colonial capital (Voorhies 280–83). In the late eighteenth and early nineteenth centuries, the Attakapas and Opelousas free black populations grew quickly, both in demographic and economic importance. By 1810, there were 269 *gens de couleur libre* in Attakapas and 380 in Opelousas (Voorhies 45).

This rapid growth—which paralleled the explosive growth of Louisiana's other free black communities—resulted in large part from the sexual imbalance in the white community. There were 1,400 white males in the Attakapas in the 1810 census but only 1,064 white females. White males twenty-six years of age or older outnumbered comparably aged white females by a margin of 727 to 583 (1810 census). A similar imbalance existed in the Opelousas district, where, in 1810, white males outnumbered white females by a substantial margin—1,746 to 1,293 (1810 census). As a consequence, white men predictably began to exploit their female slaves sexually. Some of the resulting liaisons endured for years, eventually evolving into extralegal marriages. Many such common-law wives were manumitted by their owners, particularly if they had borne children, because, under contemporary Louisiana law, natural children derived their legal status (i.e., slave or free) from their mother.

Along the southwestern Louisiana frontier, emancipated concubines usually remained a part of planters' households long after their manumission. It is thus no coincidence that the demographic profiles of early free black households in both the Opelousas and Attakapas regions generate a composite portrait of a "typical" free black household containing small numbers of white men, larger numbers of free blacks (usually the planter's black consort and several mulatto children), and still larger numbers of black slaves (Table 1).

The 1810 census of the Territory of Orleans affords abundant additional evidence of the interracial character of the early free black households in the Attakapas and Opelousas districts. According to the census of the Attakapas district, whites were the heads of forty of the sixty-seven households (59.70 percent) containing free persons of color. Twenty-four of the forty white-dominated households (60 percent) contained no white women.

This trend was far more pronounced in Attakapas than in Opelousas, where, in 1810, fifty-two of the eighty-two enumerated free black households (63 percent) were dominated by free persons of color. By 1820, the proportion of free black households headed by free blacks had

TABLE 1

Composite Views of Attakapas and Opelousas Area Households
Containing Free Blacks, 1810–1820

	Whites		FPC's		Slaves	
	No.	%	No.	%	No.	%
Attakapas						
Attakapas, 1810	189	21.16	277	31.02	427	47.82
St. Martin, 1820	104	19.29	205	38.03	230	42.67
St. Mary, 1820	122	17.81	150	21.90	413	60.29
Opelousas						
Opelousas, 1810	88	13.71	380	57.23	191	29.06
St. Landry, 1820	190	12.18	729	46.73	641	41.09

Sources: 1810 census; 1820 census.

grown to 71.43 percent. The greater independence of the Opelousas free black community stemmed in part from the greater availability of cheap land, which made economic autonomy more easily attainable, and in part from a small-scale migration of economically independent free black families from the Mississippi River parishes (1810 census, Opelousas; 1820 census, St. Landry Parish).

The 1820 census of the Attakapas and Opelousas regions demonstrates this point. White heads of households with free black occupants were most numerous in St. Mary Parish, where topography militated against land usage outside the narrow natural levees bordering the local bayous and rivers. All arable land in the parish was thus claimed and exploited far more quickly than in neighboring parishes to the north, where prairie lands supplemented the natural levees. It is thus hardly surprising that, in 1820, twenty-two of the thirty-four St. Mary Parish households containing free blacks (64.7 percent) were dominated by whites, usually white men. In neighboring St. Martin Parish, where the availability of prairie land helped reduce land prices, only twenty-four of forty-four households with free blacks (54.54 percent) were headed by whites. Finally, in St. Landry Parish, which possessed vast expanses of unclaimed prairie land, whites headed only 28.57 percent (sixteen of fifty-six) of all free black households (1820 census, St. Martin, St. Landry, and St. Mary parishes).

The number of households dominated by free black women was inversely proportional to the number of households headed by white men. As suggested above, the smallest number of female-dominated FPC households was located in the lower Teche Valley, with the highest concentration of female-dominated households in St. Landry Parish (Table 2).

The establishment of female-dominated Creole of Color households in the early antebellum period resulted from the dissolution of the common-law marriages between whites, usually white Creoles, and free black women. Many such living arrangements endured for the life of the white householder, but many, perhaps most, liaisons ended when the host planter took a white spouse. In the latter instance, the onetime black common-law wives and their natural children almost universally assumed the surname of the family's white progenitor—much to the horror of the white family. The resulting resentment was frequently exacerbated by inter vivos donations made by white men to former concubines and their natural children. At the time of, or often shortly after, their legal marriages, white men formerly involved in interracial common-law relationships frequently transferred significant amounts of money or property to their mixed-racial family—at the expense of the legitimate heirs' inheritance—and the mistress's patrimony often provided the economic basis for the family's newly elevated status in the region's three-tier social system. For example, on January 21, 1804—ap-

TABLE 2

Female-Dominated FPC Households, 1820

	Female-Dominated	Total	Percent
St. Mary Parish	1	34	2.94
St. Martin Parish	3	44	6.82
St. Landry Parish	22	56	39.29

Source: 1820 census.

proximately four years after his marriage to a white woman (Hébert 1: 214), Jacques Fontenette donated to Louise, a free black woman, and her nine mulatto children several slaves and a parcel of land measuring five arpents frontage by forty arpents depth at "Isle à Labbé" in St. Martin Parish. Seven years later, when John Palfrey purchased an adjoining tract, the public notary solemnly recorded that the property was still bounded by mulattoes, "who call themselves children of Jacques Fontenette" (St. Martin Parish, Original Acts, 26:198).

The Fontenette story is no means an isolated example (Everett 46–47). On October 30, 1806, Jean-Baptiste Carmouche willed his farm to his mulatto mistress, Marie Josephe Lalonde. Douglas Wilkins, a wealthy Opelousas-area planter, "emancipated his slave mistress, Leonora, and his acknowledged sons, Joseph Douglas and Charles Douglas, in his will. He also left his sons $3,000 and $2,000 respectively, and stipulated that they were to be sent to a free state, educated in the three 'R's,' and taught a trade. He provided Leonora with an $150 annuity" (Schafer 177). Another Opelousas resident, Augustin Belaire Fontenot, in his last will and testament, recognized and acknowledged the eight natural children born to him and his free woman of color mistress, Genevieve Hugon. In his will he provided Genevieve with a $300 annuity and a Negro slave. He gave as much of his estate to his natural children as the law allowed and the remainder to his nephew and universal heir, Jacques Dupré. The probate court awarded half of the estate to Jacques Dupré and the remainder to Genevieve and her children. On August 17, 1824, Jacques Dupré renounced one-half of the amount awarded to him by the court and donated that amount to his uncle's natural children (St. Landry Parish, Notary Book AA, pp. 48–51). The St. Martin and St. Landry parish archives, as well as the records of district civil and state supreme courts, provide evidence of dozens of such donations.

As the antebellum period progressed, however, manumission and endowment of mistresses and natural children became progressively more difficult because of increasingly stringent legal restrictions on slave emancipations and increasingly frequent adjudicatory challenges by white relatives of the manumittors. Legal historian Judith K. Schafer notes that "irate white heirs brought suits to the Louisiana Supreme Court on several occasions during the antebellum period to deny slave mistresses and their children their freedom and legacies left to them in the will of the master" (170). Matriarchal free black households consequently grew less and less common in the late antebellum period. Indeed, although interracial alliances remained a fixture in the region's cultural landscape, despite the prohibition against interracial unions in the 1825 civil code (Sterkx 243), by 1850 they constituted less than 10 percent of all FPC households in the old Opelousas district (now subdivided into St. Landry and Calcasieu parishes)—with the exception of Vermilion Parish, where there were only two free black families. Interracial unions constituted less than 15 percent of all free black households in the old Attakapas district (now consisting of St. Martin, St. Mary, Lafayette, and Vermilion parishes) (Table 3).

These interracial unions, which in the late eighteenth and early nineteenth centuries had normally been created by white Creole men and free women of color, were, in the mid-nineteenth century, more commonly established by French immigrant, Anglo-American, or Acadian/Cajun men and Creole of Color women (Table 4). Liaisons between white women and Creole of Color men were far less common; indeed, the 1850 census and the Opelousas newspapers note only a handful of such instances (*Opelousas Journal,* April 25, 1868). Yet they were nevertheless noteworthy, primarily for the violent reaction they elicited from the white community.

Second- and third-generation Creole of Color households throughout the prairie districts were consistently patriarchal because free black

TABLE 3

Heads of Households Containing Free Persons of Color, 1850 Census

Parish	No. White	Percent	No. FPC	Percent
Calcasieu	5	11.36	39	88.64
Lafayette	4	10.26	35	89.74
St. Landry	24	7.12	313	92.88
St. Martin	17	13.60	108	86.40
St. Mary	2	2.41	81	97.59
Vermilion	1	.50	1	0.50

Source: 1850 census.

TABLE 4

FPC Households Containing White Males, 1850

Parish	Foreign French	White Creole	Anglo-American	European immigrant	Acadian
Total	19	9	16	3	7
Percent	35.19	16.67	29.62	5.56	12.96
Calcasieu	0	0	5	1	0
Lafayette	3	0	0	0	2
St. Landry	9	5	9	1	2
St. Martin	5	4	2	1	3
St. Mary	2	0	0	0	0
Vermilion	0	0	0	0	0

men married within their caste and established stable nuclear families. The resulting network of blood relationships within the emerging Creole of Color caste helped bring to the community a common identity and shared values that overshadowed the subregional economic differences between individual group members (Baker and Kreamer 78–79). Undergirding this emerging group identity was their marginal status in antebellum Louisiana society, a social condition established and maintained by laws and the prevailing racial biases of the day.

CHAPTER TWO

Roots, Trunks, and Branches

Endogamy, encouraged by early Louisiana's legal and social systems, was the mechanism that sustained the emerging Creole of Color community of the prairie country. Within two generations, the region's first mulatto families had intermarried to such an extent that community and extended family boundaries virtually coincided. Indeed, interfamily relationships within Creole of Color clans are so complex that even experienced historians and genealogists experience great difficulty in tracing individuals' lines back to founding families.

This difficulty results in part from a paucity of pertinent genealogical records from the colonial period that enshrouds much early history of the Creoles of Color in the prairie parishes. Extant records, nevertheless, shed some light on the roots of the major families. These families generally shared a common heritage, forged on the southwestern Louisiana frontier in the late eighteenth century.

The Opelousas and Attakapas posts were not settled until the chaotic transitional period between the end of French rule and the beginning of Spanish dominion (ca. 1763–69), when the arrival of successive waves of land speculators, retired French military personnel, refugees from British rule in the trans-Appalachian region, and Acadian exiles carved new homes from the local wilderness. Among these new frontiersmen were Louis Ricard and his family and Gregoire Guillory, who migrated from Mobile, Alabama, to the Grand Prairie area of the Opelousas district with his two families (one mulatto and one white) sometime around 1764.

Numerous land disputes among the Opelousas and Attakapas families in the late 1760s effectively stemmed the tide of immigration. But Governor Alejandro O'Reilly's ordinance of 1770 provided renewed impetus for settlement along the western Louisiana frontier by establishing liberal guidelines for land grants: "To obtain in the Opelousas, Attakapas, and Natchitoches a grant of forty-two arpents in front by forty-two arpents in depth [approximately two and a half square miles], the applicant must [show] that he is possessor of one hundred head of tame cattle, some horses and sheep, and two slaves to look after them; a proportion which shall always be maintained in the grants to be made in the said places." This ordinance resulted in the migration of modestly wealthy but ambitious settlers from the more densely populated areas to the east and southeast—the German Coast, the Pointe Coupée district, and New Orleans. François Lemelle of the German Coast and Donato Bello of New Orleans were among those who moved to the Opelousas post with their dual (white and mulatto) families, including their Creole of Color children.

Donato Bello, an infantry officer and a native of Corand, Naples, married in New Orleans on January 15, 1765, Suzanne Moreau of Alabama, the daughter of Joseph Valentin Moreau and Marie Jean Lafleur. Their children included Catherine Bello, Maximillien Bello, Valerie Bello, Judique Bello, Sophie Bello, and Don Louis Bello (St. Landry Parish, Probate 95, Donato Bello). The first records of Donato Bello in the Opelousas and Attakapas post appear in 1787, when his daughter Catherine married Jean Alexandre Durosseau of St. Michael Parish in Bordeaux, France (Louisiana State Archives and Record Service, Opelousas Colonial Records).

Donato Bello obviously maintained a simultaneous relationship with Marie Jeanne Talliaferro, a New Orleans–born mulatto. Talliaferro bore Bello at least three children—Martin, Marie Céleste, and Catherine Victoire. These children first appear in the documentary record of the Opelousas post on November 3, 1789, with the signing of a marriage contract between Catherine Victoire and Jean-Baptiste Guillory, a native of the Opelousas post and the natural son of Gregoire Guillory and Marguerite, a free Negress (Original Acts, Sabatier Collection). According to the document, both Gregoire Guillory and Donato Bello were deceased. Martin Donato signed the document as a witness for his sister. Land grant records indicate that Jean-Baptiste Guillory was Martin Donato's stock keeper on property Martin owned along Bayou Mallet (now designated as section 44 of Township 7 South, Range 1 West, and

**Free Black Landholdings
in the Swords Area of St. Landry Parish,
Early Nineteenth Century**

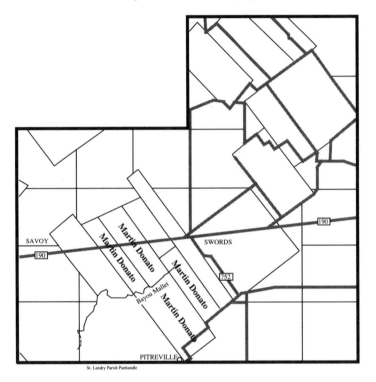

St. Landry Parish Panhandle

section 45 of Townships 7 and 8 South, Range 1 West). Under the terms of the O'Reilly ordinance, Jean-Baptiste also assisted his wife, Catherine Victoire, in securing a grant which is now designated as section 43 of Township 7 South, Range 1 West (State Land Office Records).

Marie Céleste Donato first appears in the records of the Opelousas post on February 6, 1796, when she entered into a marriage contract with Jean-Baptiste Meuillon, a native of the parish of St. Charles on the German Coast and the natural son of François Cheval and Marie Anne Meuillon, a free Negress (Vidrine and De Ville 40). According to the marriage contract, Marie Céleste owned twelve arpents of land at Bois Mallet. This tract, containing twelve arpents front by forty arpents depth, is now designated as section 40 of Township 7 South, Range 1 West (State Land Office Records). In this marriage contract, Martin

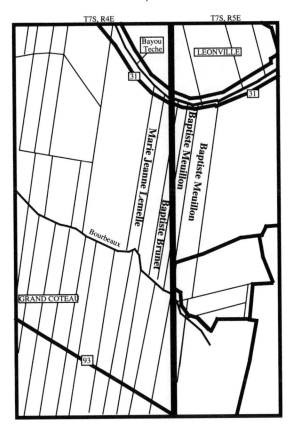

T7S, R4E   T7S, R5E

Bayou Teche

LEONVILLE

31

31

Marie Jeanne Lemelle

Baptiste Meuillon

Baptiste Meuillon

Baptiste Brunet

Bourbeaux

GRAND COTEAU

93

Early Antebellum Free Black Landholdings
in the Prairie Laurent/Leonville Area

Donato signed as a witness for the groom rather than for his sister. The groom, who referred to himself as Baptiste Meuillon, indicated that he had secured an order of settlement on a tract of land where he had already established a home in which his future spouse resided. This tract, near present-day Leonville on Bayou Teche, is now identified as Section 22, Township 7 South, Range 5 East (State Land Office Records).

Martin Donato, the patriarch of the Donato clan, entered into a common-law relationship with Marianne Duchesne, the natural daughter of Louis Duchesne and Nanette St. Laurent, a Negress and a native of New Orleans, sometime in the 1780s. By the time they entered into

**Landholdings of
Free Persons of Color
Opelousas Area
Early Nineteenth Century**

TOWNSHIP 6 SOUTH, RANGE 4 EAST
(IN THE OPELOUSAS DISTRICT)

a marriage contract on March 16, 1803, they had had six children: Lucien Martin, Marie Denise, Marie Louise, Martin Antoine Celestin, Céleste Emelie, and Augustin Donat (Vidrine and De Ville 64). In fact, by the time Martin and Marianne were married, two of their children, Martin Antoine Celestin (Martin Donato, *fils*) and Marie Denise, were already married.

In the marriage contract Martin Donato indicated that he owned a *vacherie* (cattle ranch) in Bois Mallet containing twenty arpents frontage on both sides of the Coulee de Senneliers with a depth of forty-two arpents (this is the tract mentioned above as Jean-Baptiste Guillory's place of employment). Located on the land was the herder's cabin, a building twenty-two feet long by sixteen feet wide. In addition to the *vacherie,* Donato also indicated that he owned a plantation where he and Marianne resided. This tract of land he described as being eleven arpents front by forty-two arpents depth. His residence was a house built on the ground, measuring fifty feet plus porches. On his plantation he had just installed a new cotton mill. The work force for his plantation consisted of his three adult sons and three adult male slaves. The original claimant of the land composing this plantation was Baptiste Fontenot, who evidently sold it to Martin Donato before March 1803 (State Land Office Records).

Among Martin Donato's movable possessions were 150 head of four-year-old beef cattle, 450 horned cattle, male and female of all ages, and 26 horses. He also indicated that his cash assets were $5,000 piastres, some of which were loaned out. He evidently had already begun a practice he would continue throughout his life, that of serving as a private banker to his neighbors, both whites and Creoles of Color.

An analysis of the marriage contracts of the Opelousas post demonstrates that the separate properties listed by Martin Donato and Marianne Duchesne, valued in excess of twenty thousand piastres, far exceeded in value the possessions declared by any other Opelousas post residents—either white or black—entering into marriage contracts during the colonial period (Vidrine and DeVille).

The Donato family's experiences greatly resemble those of the Lemelles. François Lemelle, like the progenitor of the Donato clan, capitalized on the O'Reilly ordinance by moving from the German Coast to the Opelousas post with his wife, Charlotte Labbé, and his children, Jacques, François Denis, and Marie Louise, the wife of Jean-Baptiste Boutté of Attakapas. François also brought his Creole of Color family to the Opelousas frontier. His relationship with Marie Jeanne Davion Lemelle produced at least three sons and three daughters, François, Louis, Hildebert, Julie, Jacqueline, and Catherine. The marriage, on March 1, 1802, of François Lemelle to Marie Denise Donato, the daughter of Martin Donato and Marianne Duchesne, began the union of the two families. That union was extended later that year when, on July 27, 1802, Hildebert Lemelle married Marie Louise Allain, the daughter of Marianne Duchesne born before her cohabitation with Martin Donato. The marriage of Marie Jeanne's other son, Louis, on October 16, 1798, to Céleste Olympe Grandpré, the sister of Valerien Auzenne, added yet another family name to the increasingly complex family network. Valerien Auzenne was already a member of the household of Louis's half-brother Denis Lemelle. Thus by the end of the Spanish colonial period, the families of Donato, Meuillon, Guillory, Lemelle, and Auzenne had already forged the bonds they would later tighten through continued intermarriage.

Over the next few years the families appear to have prospered. By 1817, Marie Jeanne Lemelle owned 240 acres of second-quality land on Bayou Teche as well as 800 acres of first-quality land along the area's principal waterway. Her movable possessions included five slaves. Baptiste Meuillon was the owner of 800 acres of first-quality land plus 480 acres of second-quality land, all on Bayou Teche. His movable property included twenty-six slaves, thirty horses and mules, and two hundred horned cattle. By the following year he had increased his slaveholdings to thirty-three, an increase of eighteen slaves from the fifteen reported in the 1810 census (St. Landry Parish, Tax Rolls, 1817, 1818).

When Jean-Baptiste Guillory married Catherine Victoire Donato, his total estate consisted of several cows and pack animals valued at two hundred piastres. Guillory assisted his wife, who had sixty horned cattle and ten horses bearing her brand at the time of their marriage, in securing a Spanish land grant under the O'Reilly ordinance. That grant consisted of approximately 245 acres (State Land Office Records). By 1817, Jean-Baptiste Guillory had increased his landholdings to 1,460 acres. His movable property included 4 slaves, 25 horses and mules, and 200 horned cattle. By the following year he had increased his landholdings to 1,480 acres, and his herd had grown to 275 horned cattle (St. Landry Parish, Tax Rolls, 1817).

When Martin Donato and Marianne Duchesne entered into their marriage contract on March 3, 1803, he was already a large landowner with approximately 1,820 acres (2,142 arpents). By 1817, he had increased his landholdings to 4,016 acres. His movable property included 49 slaves, 50 horses and mules, and 650 horned cattle. During the next year, he acquired several other tracts of land, including half interest in a tract which he and the widow of Michael Prudhomme bought jointly from the Prudhomme estate. The tract was 32 arpents front by 40 arpents depth for a total of 1,280 arpents or 1,088 acres. Martin's half

Land Claims of
Free Persons of Color
near Washington, Louisiana

amounted to 544 acres, while his share of the cost of the property was $1,182 (St. Landry Parish, Probate 93, Michael Prudhomme). By the time the tax assessor completed his assessments for 1818, Martin Donato's landholdings totaled 5,096 acres in Church Prairie, Gradnigo Island, Bayou Teche, Mallet, Grand Bois, and Prairie Basse. His movable property included sixty slaves—an increase of eleven in one year—while his livestock holdings remained static (St. Landry Parish, Tax Roll, 1818).

Martin Donato maintained his position as both head of the Donato clan and a member of the Donato Bello family. Although he had long since stopped using Bello as part of his name, he continued to be involved in the affairs of his white half-brothers and sisters. After the death

Land Claim of
Marie Jeanne Lemelle
along Bayou Courtableau

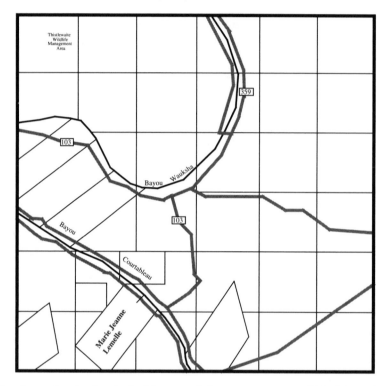

by drowning in the Atchafalaya on February 24, 1814, of his thirty-six-year-old half-brother Maximillien Bello, Martin Donato became the representative of his orphaned nephews and nieces at family conferences. One such conference occurred on January 6, 1818, when Suzanne Moreau Bello agreed to turn over the entire estate of Donato Bello to his heirs in exchange for a usufruct of the house and approximately four acres of land that surrounded the house as well as the usufruct of all of the woodland for the remainder of her life. At the sale that resulted from this conference, on January 26, 1818, one of the heirs, Don Louis Bello, purchased a thirty-one-year-old slave named Narcisse for $1,500 with Valerie Roy standing security for Don Louis. Another heir, Valerie Bello, bought a twenty-one-year-old slave named Eugene for $1,580 and his brother Don Louis signed as security. The third slave, a thirty-five-year-old man named Jean-Baptiste, was sold to Martin Donato for $1,585. Considering Martin Donato's wealth and social position at this time, it is not surprising that no security was required by the estate. The six-arpent by eighty-arpent tract of land was sold to Louis Fontenot, Suzanne Moreau Bello's neighbor, for $3,500, with no security required. Although no tableau exists for the separation of the proceeds of this sale, one must assume that Martin Donato performed his responsibilities toward his charges, the minor children of Maximillien Bello, and saw to it that their share, $1,360, was properly administered for their benefit (St. Landry Parish, Probate 95, Donato Bello).

In addition to providing evidence of the relative prosperity of the first generation of the Donato, Meuillon, Guillory, and Lemelle clans, the 1817 and 1818 tax rolls demonstrate that the second generation was already beginning to make its presence known. The records indicate that François Lemelle, Martin Donato's son-in-law, owned 168 acres of first-quality land at Church Prairie together with one slave and twenty-five horned cattle. His brother Louis Lemelle owned 160 acres of first-quality land on Bayou Courtableau and two slaves. Casimir Rougeau, the son-in-law of Jean-Baptiste and Victoire Guillory, owned 160 acres of second-quality land at Mallet, plus twenty-five horses and mules. Another son-in-law of Jean-Baptiste and Victoire, Jean Allain, owned 120 acres in Mallet, twelve horses, and twenty-five head of horned cattle.

Although both Martin Donato and Baptiste Meuillon owned land in Mallet, they made their residence along Bayou Teche and depended on Jean-Baptiste Guillory and his family to tend the cattle and land at Mallet. The journey from their residences on Bayou Teche to their holdings in Mallet, although only approximately forty miles in a direct line, was a two- or three-day trip one way on horseback and even longer by wagon and oxen. The Teche, however, provided easy access to the area along Bayou Courtableau and the Atchafalaya, including Pointe Coupée, as well as the Attakapas post along the lower Teche. As a result, several second-generation members of both the Donato and Meuillon families sought spouses among themselves, with the Lemelles near Bayou Courtableau, or with Creole of Color residents of the Attakapas post or the Pointe Coupée post. For example, Lucien Donato married Manette Balque, originally from Pointe Coupée; Auguste Donato married his first cousin Marie Denyse Meuillon; Marie Louise Donato married Attakapas native Hilaire Frilot; and Marie Denise Donato married François Lemelle. All of Baptiste Meuillon's children married their Donato and Lemelle cousins of the second and third generations.

Because they were geographically isolated at Bois Mallet, the children of Jean-Baptiste Guillory and Victoire Donato either married their Guillory cousins or other Creole of Color residents of the Bois or Prairie Mallet areas. Some of the spouses were natives of other areas who had moved to the prairie during the Spanish colonial period. For instance, Marie Céleste Guillory married Casimir Rougeau, a native of New Orleans but then a resident of Mallet; Jean-Baptiste married Marguerite Caraboye, whose mother was a Guillory; Caliste Guillory married Jean Allain, a native of Pointe Coupée and a resident of Mallet; Louis Denis Guillory married Marie Anne Papillon, a resident of Mallet; Louis Casimir Guillory married Sidonie Thierry, a resident of Mallet; and Donat Guillory married his cousin Françoise Guillory. We find the third-generation Guillorys marrying their Thierry, Papillon, Allain, Simien, or Guillory cousins.

Evidently, many of these were marriages of convenience, the parents seeking spouses for their children from among their relatives and neighbors to tighten family bonds and maintain or consolidate family landholdings. The case of Jean-Baptiste Guillory, *fils,* and his wife, Marguerite Carabaillo (Caraboye), illustrates a problem common to such marriages. Although Marguerite bore five children to Jean-Baptiste, she evidently was not satisfied with her role as wife and mother, for she began an illicit relationship with George Simien. Shortly before his death, Jean-Baptiste initiated a divorce suit against Marguerite, charging her with adultery and requesting that the court grant his divorce and assign the children of the marriage to his care because she had proven herself unfit to be their mother. The testimony in the case upheld Jean-Baptiste's allegations, and the court granted him a divorce and custody of his children (St. Landry Parish, Civil District Suit 1515).

Upon Jean-Baptiste's death a few months later, his daughter Baptistine petitioned the court to assign her uncle Evariste Guillory as her *curator ad bona* and as tutor to her minor siblings, "her mother, Marguerite Carabayo, having forfeited the tutorship of her children in consequence of having committed adultery." The court granted her petition, and Evariste assumed responsibility for his nephews and nieces, in addition to his own growing family (St. Landry Parish, Probate 516).

The probate and succession records provide a picture of the relative prosperity of the deceased as well as the means of disposition for the estate, either by inheritance or by succession sale, frequently to family members. The successions of François Donato, Valerien Auzenne, and Martin Donato are illustrative. When François Donato, the son of Martin Donato and Marianne Duchesne, died in late 1837 or early January 1838, he left an estate containing a tract of land four arpents front by eighty arpents deep with a dwelling and sugar house, as well as six slaves. The estimated value of his estate was $8,739.95. At the sale of the slaves which resulted from this succession, all but one were purchased by relatives. Donato's first cousin Evariste Guillory purchased a thirty-six-year-old male slave named Ben for $1,000. His father, Martin Donato, purchased a thirty-six-year-old female slave named Céleste, together with her three children, Valin, aged seven years, Philip, aged five years, and Valcour, aged six months. The price bid for the entire family was $1,670 (St. Landry Parish, Probate 845).

Valerien Auzenne died in 1843, and his wife, Marie Louise Gallot, died the following year. His oldest son, Carlostin, was designated as the executor of the estate, which contained a tract of land thirteen arpents front by fifty arpents depth, as well as three slaves. The estimated value of the estate was $5,130. At the estate sale, one of the heirs, Felix Auzenne, was joined by two of his cousins, Alexandre Auzenne and Martin Lemelle, in purchasing the land. Alexandre Auzenne paid the estate $330 for a male slave named Zenon. Martin Lemelle paid $885 for a mulatto woman slave named Irene. Two of the heirs, Carlostin and Felix, along with Alexandre Auzenne, Martin Lemelle, and Firmin Lemelle, paid the estate $150 for a fifty-year-old mulatto woman slave named Clarisa (St. Landry Parish, Probate 1282). The property, both real and chattel, evidently remained in the family.

Although the Martin Donato succession is discussed in Chapter 4, there are some elements of the succession that are extremely difficult and require scrutiny here. In his last will and testament Donato made financial arrangements for, and ordered the emancipation of, his slave concubine and enslaved natural children. Although he made no financial arrangements for these slaves, he ordered the emancipation of Leon, the nineteen-year-old mulatto son of his deceased son Edmond and Martin's slave Rosine. He also emancipated twin sisters Meurice and Olympie, as well as Olympie's young daughter Marie Jeanne. Approximately thirty-seven years earlier he had emancipated their brother Sabin Donato while he was still an infant. The will gives no hint as to the identity of the twin sisters' parents. A document filed by Martin Donato in October 1842 indicates that Sabin's mother was Martin's slave Céleste. That document informed Sabin of his age and baptism day and provided a guarantee that he had indeed been freed as an infant. On the strength of that document, Judge George King issued manumission papers to Sabin (St. Landry Parish, Microfile 017115). Both these documents and the will leave the paternity of Sabin, Meurice, and Olympie a mystery. Obviously they were Donato children, but whose? When Sabin Donato died in 1860, he had been preceded in death by his sister Meurice. Her three orphaned children, Anais, Valentin, and Marie, under the protection of Auguste Donato, one of Martin Donato's last surviving sons and the executor of Martin's estate, filed suit against Sabin's widow for their share of his estate. Sabin Donato had died intestate and without issue, but his widow attempted to claim the entire estate as though there were no collateral heirs (St. Landry Parish, Probate 2316). It is somewhat ironic that although Martin designated Auguste as the tutor of Julie's children, he made no such provision for Meurice and Olympie. A family council in 1860 assigned the same responsibility to Auguste for Meurice's children.

Martin Donato's life demonstrates the opportunities available to Creoles of Color in the Opelousas and Attakapas frontiers. It also demonstrates how thoroughly the Creoles of Color accepted the established economic system. During his lifetime Donato accumulated over 5,000 acres of land and at the end of his life still possessed 4,391 acres. In 1841 he sold half of the *vacherie* at Mallet, which the Guillorys had tended for him, to his nephew Evariste Guillory for $500 (St. Landry Parish, Conveyance Book IJ -1, p. 519). When he signed his marriage contract in 1803, he owned only five slaves. But he also had only about 200 acres in production and required little labor beyond that provided by his sons. As Martin Donato increased his production acreage, his need for labor grew correspondingly. We consequently find him with eigh-

Free Black Properties
in the Frilot Cove Area

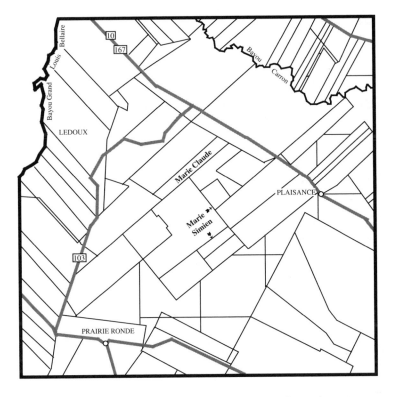

teen slaves in 1810, forty-nine slaves in 1817, sixty-three slaves in 1820, seventy-five slaves in 1830, and eighty-eight slaves when he died in 1847. The estimative inventory of his possessions appraised his 4,391 acres of land at only $6,000, less than $2 per acre. His slave property was valued at $30,000. He also had $3,705.70 in cash in his bedroom. His movable property was valued at $4,000. But the bulk of his estate, $52,914.84, was in collectible notes, most of which were secured by mortgages. Obviously, the practice of serving as banker to his Creole of Color and white neighbors continued until his death (St. Landry Parish, Probate 1339). Donato left his descendants a magnificent heritage of success against the odds. His African descent did not prevent him from forcing the economic system to grant him the recognition he deserved. Rather than cursing the system, he chose to live within it and forced it to work to his advantage and to the advantage of his successors.

CHART 1

The Natural Children of Donato Bello and Marie-Jeanne Taillefero, a mulatresse of New Orleans

1. Martin Donato Bello married Marianne Duchesne, the natural daughter of Louis Duchesne and Nanette St. Laurent, a Negress of New Orleans. [Marianne Duchesne had also lived in Pointe Coupée.]

2. Céleste Donato Bello married Jean-Baptiste Meuillon, natural son of François Cheval, from the parish of St. Charles, and Marie Anne Meuillon, *negresse libre.*

3. Victoire Donato Bello married Jean-Baptiste Guillory, the natural son of Gregoire Guillory, and Marguerite, *negresse libre.*

Note: Although all three identified themselves as the children of Donato Bello in their marriage contracts, neither Marie Céleste nor Victoire used the name Bello. Martin signed as Martin Donato in his sisters' contracts, although for his own he signed M. Donato Bello. Sometime between 1803 and 1818, he dropped the Bello from his name. Thereafter he signed either Martin Donato or M. Donato.

CHART 2

The Natural Children of François Lemelle and Marie Jeanne Davion Lemelle

1. François Donato Lemelle, who, on March 1, 1802, married Marie Denise Donato, daughter of Martin Donato and Marianne Duchesne. *Their children are listed in Chart 3, number 7, A through N.*

2. Louis Lemelle, who, on October 16, 1798, married Céleste Olympe Grandpré, a native of Pointe Coupée and the natural daughter of Charles Grandpré and Jeanette Glapion.

   Their children were

   A. Louis Lemelle, *fils,* who married Céleste Adelaide Lessassier on February 12, 1831.

Their child was

1) Marie Louise Lemelle, who, on December 8, 1857, married her first cousin Joseph Delmont Donato, son of Edmond Donato, *père,* and Aimée Gradenigo.

B. Charles Lemelle, who, on May 31, 1836, married his first cousin Euphemie Lemelle, daughter of François Lemelle and Marie Denise Donato.

Their children are listed in Chart 3, number 7, A.

3. Hildebert Lemelle, who on July 27, 1802, married Marie Louise Allain of Pointe Coupée, the natural daughter of Marianne Duchesne.

Their child was

A. Alfred Lemelle, who, on April 15, 1831, married Adelaide Lessassier of St. Charles Parish.

4. Julie Lemelle, who, on July 21, 1786, married Jean Gallot, the son of Jean Gallot and Marguerite Mezevida, native of Bordeaux in Guienne.

Their child was

A. Henriette Gallot, baptized October 13, 1787.

5. Jacqueline

6. Catherine

CHART 3

The Children of Martin Donato and Marianne Duchesne

1. Antoine Martin Celestin Donato, *dit* Martin Donato, *fils,* married April 21, 1800, Marianne Castillon.

Their child was

A. Bello Auguste Donato, who on September 24, 1852, married his first cousin Leocadie Lemelle, the daughter of Marie Denise Donato and François Lemelle, *père.*

After Marianne Castillon died, Martin Donato, *fils,* married Ann [Manette] Paillet.

Their child was

A. Celonise [Sydalise] Céleste Donato, who on July 9, 1845, married Edouard Fuselier.

After Martin Donato, *fils,* died, Ann Paillet married Louis Frilot.

2. Lucien Donate [Donato], *père,* married February 12, 1811, Manette Balque, the daughter of James Balque and Marie Françoise Laurens of Pointe Coupée.

Their children were

A. Lucien Donato, *fils.* He was baptized in 1816. He never married and died without issue. His sister's children inherited his estate.

B. Eliza [Elizabeth] Donato, who on April 5, 1831, married her second cousin Antoine Donato Meuillon, the son of Jean-Baptiste Meuillon and Céleste Donato.

Their children were

1) Antoine Alphonse Meuillon, who, on September 23, 1858, married his second cousin Marie Meuillon, the daughter of François Meuillon and Marie Françoise Lemelle.

2) Ann Elizabeth Meuillon, who, on February 15, 1851, married Auguste Belaire. After his death, she remarried, on May 19, 1855, Simon Birotte, the son of François Birotte and Elise Guillory.

3) Céleste Armentine Meuillon, who, on February 7, 1857, married Pierre Elicio Frilot, the son of Antoine Frilot and Adelaide Frilot.

4) Marie Clementine Meuillon, who, on November 15, 1859, married Jacques C. Auzenne, the son of Edmond Auzenne and Chalinette DeBlanc.

5) Lucien Terrance Meuillon

6) Leocadie Meuillon, who, on July 30, 1861, married Jules Pierre Frilot, the son of Philippe Frilot and Emelie Fuselier.

7) Jean-Baptiste Armand Meuillon

3. Auguste [Augustin] Donat, who, on December 4, 1827, married his first cousin Marie Denise Meuillon, the daughter of Jean-Baptiste Meuillon and Céleste Donato.

Their children were

A. Auguste Donato, *fils,* who, on May 12, 1853, married his first cousin Clara Donate (Donato), the daughter of François Donate (Donato) and Céleste (Celestine) Dobbs (Daube).

Their children were

1) François Auguste Donato, born March 3, 1854.

2) Marie Felicie Donato, born November 20, 1855.

3) Charles Rigobert Donato, born January 4, 1862.

B. Gustave Meuillon Donato, who married Marie Anne Emelie (Amelia) Lessassier, the daughter of Jean Lessassier and Eleanor Ritren, on April 18, 1855.

Their child was

1) Marie Susanne Frederick, born January 4, 1856.

4. François Donate (Donato), who married Céleste (Celestine) Dobbs (Daube) on November 15, 1819.

Their children were

A. Colomb Donate (Donato), who married Euphrasie Lemelle

Their child was François Alcide Donato.

B. Clara Donate (Donato), who married her first cousin Auguste Donato, *fils,* on May 12, 1853.

Their children are listed under 3. A. above.

C. Marie Louise Donate (Donato), who, on November 30, 1843, married her first cousin Rigobert Lemelle, the son of François Lemelle and Marie Denise Donato.

D. Emelie Donate (Donato), who married Emile Lemelle on May 26, 1846.

Their children were

1) Elisée Lemelle

2) Cassius Lemelle

3) Elizabeth Lemelle

After his death she entered into a second marriage with Virgile Esterling on June 11, 1857.

E. Celestine Donate (Donato), who married Sosthene Auzenne on September 12, 1849.

5. Edmond Donate (Donato), who, on February 8, 1831, married Aimée Gradenigo, the daughter of Joseph Gradenigo and Adelaide Lemelle.

   Their children were

   A. Edmond Donato, *fils,* born January 3, 1831.

   B. Cornelius Donato, who married Victorine Follain on December 2, 1856.

   C. Joseph Delmont Donato, who married Marie Louise Lemelle on December 8, 1857.

6. Marie Louise Donate (Donato), who, on August 4, 1812, married Louis Hilaire Frilot of Attakapas, the son of Claude Frilot and Rosalie Boutté of New Orleans and Attakapas.

   Their child was

   A. Marie Louise Frilot, who, on July 24, 1839, married her first cousin Ludger Lemelle, the son of François Lemelle and Marie Denise Donato.

After Ludger's death, she married his brother, also her first cousin, François Lemelle, *fils,* on February 11, 1850.

7. Marie Denise Donate (Donato), who, on March 1, 1802, married François Lemelle, the natural son of Marie Jeanne Davion Lemelle and François Lemelle.

   Their children were

   A. Euphemie Lemelle, who, on May 31, 1836, married her first cousin Charles Lemelle, the son of Louis Lemelle and Céleste Grandpré.

      Their children were

      1) Charles Lemelle, *fils,* born August 20, 1837.

      2) Cecile Lemelle, who, on May 25, 1860 married Louis Frilot, the son of Louis Frilot and Ann Paillet, the widow of Martin Donato *fils.*

B. Marianne Lemelle, who married Felix Auzenne on April 23, 1844.

C. Firmin Lemelle, who, on December 20, 1836, married Céleste (Celanie) Auzenne (Ozenne), the daughter of Valerien Auzenne and Marie Louise Gallot.

Their children were

1) Nicomede Lemelle, born September 15, 1849.

2) Henri Lemelle, born July 8, 1855.

D. François Lemelle, *fils,* who, on February 11, 1850, married his first cousin Marie Louise Frilot, the daughter of Louis Hilaire Frilot and Marie Louise Donato. She was also the widow of his brother Ludger Lemelle.

E. Marie Françoise Lemelle, who married her second cousin François Meuillon on July 12, 1831.

Their children were

1) Marie Meuillon, who, on September 22, 1858, married her second cousin Antoine Alphonse Meuillon, the son of Antoine Donato Meuillon and Eliza Donato.

2) Josephine Meuillon, who, on July 12, 1859, married Agenor Lessassier. Josephine died on May 26, 1862.

F. Ludger Lemelle, who, on July 25, 1839, married his first cousin Marie Louise Frilot, the daughter of Louis Hilaire Frilot and Marie Louise Donato.

G. Rigobert Lemelle, who, on November 30, 1843, married his first cousin Marie Louise Donato, the daughter of François Donato and Céleste Dobbs.

Their children were

1) Hubert Lemelle, who died at age twelve on January 12, 1860.

2) Céleste Lemelle, born January 24, 1854.

3) Corinne Lemelle, who died at age fourteen on January 30, 1863.

4) Paulin Rigobert Lemelle, who died at age six months on April 28, 1865.

H. Martin Lemelle, who married Marie Ann Auzenne on February 6, 1844

Their children were

1) Martin Lemelle, Jr., born December 25, 1851.

2) Rodolphe Lemelle, born March 16, 1854.

I. Leocadie Lemelle, who, on September 28, 1852, married her first cousin Bello Auguste Donato, the son of Martin Donato, *fils,* and Marianne Castillon.

J. Marie Elodie Lemelle, who married Hilaire Paillet on May 30, 1848.

K. Eloy Lemelle, who died at age thirty-eight years on July 27, 1863.

L. Alexandre Leo Lemelle, who married Marie Ann Teracine Meuillon on May 4, 1852.

M. Leon Lemelle.

N. Catherine Lemelle.

CHART 4

The Children of Catherine Victoire Donato and Jean-Baptiste Guillory

1. Marie Céleste Guillory was baptized on September 25, 1795, and married Casimir Rougeau of New Orleans on May 17, 1811.

Their children were

A. Victoire Rougeau, who, on February 7, 1832, married Joachim (Joasin) Guillory.

Their children were

1) Joseph Guillory, who was born on July 8, 1841. He married, on October 30, 1865, Marie Eloise Simien, the daughter of George Simien and Genevieve Guillory.

2) Joachim Guillory, *fils,* who, on December 8, 1851, married Emelie Joubert, the daughter of Jacob Joubert and Céleste Damas.

3) Joachine Guillory, who, on March 3, 1859, married her second cousin Casimir Guillory, *fils,* the son of Casimir Guillory and Sidonie Thierry.

4) Celestine Guillory, who, on September 8, 1859, married Auguste Papillon, the son of Alexandre Papillon and Brigitte Pars.

5) Firmin Guillory, who, on December 18, 1860, married Elizabeth Allain, the daughter of Auguste Allain and Elizabeth Jardoin.

Their child was

Firmin Colin Guillory, born March 6, 1862

6) Christine Bridget Guillory, who, on December 28, 1863, married Joseph Guillory, *fils,* the son of Joseph Guillory and Marie Anne Papillon.

B. Israel Rougeau, who, on January 6, 1863, married Ulcher Allain, the son of Auguste Allain and Elizabeth Jardoin.

C. Silvanie Rougeau, who, on May 15, 1860, married Zepherin Birotte, the son of François Birotte and Elise Guillory.

2. Jean-Baptiste Guillory, *fils,* who, on April 27, 1813, married Marguerite Caraboye (Caramail, Carabaillo), the daughter of Julien Caraboye and Marie Guillory of Pensacola.

Their children were

A. Baptistine Guillory, who, on November 12, 1838, married Thomas Collins.

B. Jean-Baptiste Guillory, who was born on November 2, 1816.

C. Adeline Guillory, who, on November 16, 1840, married Francis William Carrol.

D. Julien Guillory, who, on October 9, 1838, married Marie Louise Victoriane.

Their child was

Florentine Guillory, who was born on November 24, 1855

E. David Guillory, who, on September 30, 1842, married Caroline Papillon.

Their child was

Michael Guillory, who was born on November 21, 1855

Note: Jean-Baptiste, *fils,* died either late in 1829 or very early in 1830. His brother Evariste, on January 27, 1830, was appointed *curator ad bona* for Baptistine and tutor to the others, all minors.

3. Caliste Guillory was born on July 8, 1793. On January 22, 1811, she married Jean Allain of Pointe Coupée

Their child was

   A. Aurelien Allain, who, on June 12, 1845, married his first cousin Marianne Guillory, the daughter of Evariste Guillory and Marie Anne Ford.

4. Louis Denis Guillory, who married Marie Anne Verseinde Papillon on October 8, 1816.

Their children were

   A. Demaitre Denis Guillory, who, on November 23, 1843, married Marie Louise Guillory, the daughter of Joseph Guillory and Louise Tessier. After her death, Demaitre married, on December 17, 1860, Elina Verret, the daughter of Pierre Verret and Arco Allain.

   B. Marianne Guillory, who, on October 23, 1845, married Onesime Guillory, the son of Joseph Guillory and Eloise Meuillon.

   C. Adolph Guillory, who, on August 12, 1852, married Augustine Guillory, the daughter of François Guillory and Athenaise Guillory.

   D. Melite Guillory, who, on July 22, 1851, married François Guillory, *fils,* the son of François Guillory and Adelaide Guillory.

      After Denis's death Marie Anne married Joseph Guillory, *fils,* on February 10, 1838.

5. Louis Casimir Guillory was born April 24, 1807. He married Sidonie (Cydonise) Thierry (Thiery) on August 12, 1836.

Their children were

A. Michael Laissin Guillory was born on September 29, 1838. He married, on April 19, 1860, Bernardine Thierry, the daughter of Alexandre Thierry and Clementine Thierry.

B. Casimir Guillory, *fils*, who, on March 3, 1851, married his second cousin Joachine Guillory, the daughter of Joachim Guillory and Victoire Rougeau

C. Sidonie Guillory, who, on April 10, 1860, married her first cousin Isaac Guillory, the son of Evariste Guillory and Marie Anne Ford.

D. Sidonie Casimir Guillory, who was born on April 8, 1854, and died on April 28, 1857.

E. Augustin Guillory, who, on July 13, 1863, married Agnes Mirthe Guillory, the daughter of Martin Guillory and Louise Forstall.

6. Evariste Guillory. Although no record of marriage could be found, he evidently had a long-standing relationship with Marie Anne Ford, which resulted in several children.

A. Marianne Guillory, who, on June 12, 1845, married her first cousin Aurelien Allain, the son of Jean Allain and Caliste Guillory.

B. Victoire Guillory, who, on December 19, 1851, married Julien Gallot, the son of Jean Gallot and Françoise Brunet.

C. Isaac Guillory, who, on April 4, 1855, married Marie Francillette Guillory, the daughter of François Guillory and Athenaise Guillory.

After her death, Isaac married, on March 11, 1860, his first cousin Sidonie Guillory, the daughter of Casimir Guillory and Sidonie Thierry.

D. Evariste Guillory, *fils*, who, on August 6, 1858, married Louisa Armentine Guillory, the daughter of François Guillory and Athenaise Guillory.

After Marie Anne Ford's death, Evariste, *père*, married, on April 19, 1860, Marie Louise Alexandre, the daughter of Alexandre and Helene (no last names in the record)

7. Marie Louise Guillory, who, on November 9, 1824, married François Birot (Birotte) of New Orleans, the son of François Birot (Birotte) and Julie Dobegne.

8. Donat (Donato) Guillory, who, on June 10, 1850, married Françoise Guillory.

Their child was

> Catherine Victoire Guillory, who, on December 7, 1863, married Martin Cleophas Guillory, the son of Martin Guillory and Marie Ann Forstall.

CHART 5

The Children of Jean-Baptiste Meuillon (the natural son of Marie Anne Meuillon, *negresse libre,* and François Cheval) and Céleste Donato Bello (the natural daughter of Marie-Jeanne Taillefero, mulatress, native of New Orleans, and Sieur Donato Bello, infantry officer)

1. Antoine Donato Meuillon, who, on April 5, 1831, married his second cousin Elizabeth (Eliza) Donato, the daughter of Lucien Donato, *père,* and Manette Balque.

Their children are listed in Chart 3, number 2, B.

2. François Meuillon, who, on July 12, 1831, married his second cousin Marie Françoise Lemelle, the daughter of François Lemelle, *père,* and Marie Denise Donato.

Their children are listed in Chart 3, number 7, E.

3. Marie Denyse Meuillon, who, on December 4, 1827, married her first cousin Auguste Donato, the son of Martin Donato and Marianne Duchesne.

Their children are listed in Chart 3, number 3.

CHART 6

The Natural Children of Martin Donato and Julie, his slave

1. Eugenie Donato, who, on January 15, 1861, married Leon Manse.

2. Emile Donato

3. Uranie Donato

4. Felicianne Donato

5. Felicie Donato, who, on July 25, 1861, married Louis B. Cuny.

6. Philomene Donato

7. Didier Donato, who died in Alexandria on December 24, 1864.

Sources: Hébert, Vols. 1–7 and 33; Louisiana State Archives, Opelousas Colonial Records; George Sabatier Collection, Opelousas Colonial Records; St. Landry Parish Courthouse.

CHAPTER THREE

Antebellum Economic, Social, and Legal Realities

Beginning with the promulgation of the Code Noir (Black Code) in 1724, Louisiana's legal system fostered the creation and maintenance of a three-tier social system, with a white elite and a black servile population at the polar extremes and, between them, a free black class that enjoyed most of the legal rights and privileges, but not the social status, of whites (Allain 127–37). The colonial and antebellum records of the Attakapas and Opelousas posts list a surprising number of conveyances between whites and free persons of color, both men and women; conveyances between free persons of color; business contracts between whites and free Negroes, as well as between free men of color; suits by whites against free blacks; suits involving only *gens de couleur libre;* suits by free blacks against whites; and marriage contracts between free Negroes. These legal instruments clearly show that free blacks were fully aware of their legal rights and responsibilities, that they knew how to use the legal system effectively to protect their civil and property rights, and that they were full participants in the region's economic system. Marriage contracts between free persons of color dating from the late 1770s in the Opelousas area and including most of the early Creole of Color families (e.g., the Donato, Meuillon, Lemelle, Charlot, Decuir, Chevis, Grandpré, Lenormand, Lesassier, Masse, and Simien families) in particular indicate both the extent to which the *gens de couleur libre* were part of the system and their effectiveness in using it to their advantage.

The region's social system, however, was far less congenial to free people of color. Although the administrative and civil records indicate that from the 1770s through the early antebellum period, whites and blacks often traveled together between the Teche Valley and New Orleans, sometimes aboard cramped pirogues, the social gap between the two groups was difficult, if not impossible, to bridge. Such mixed racial traveling companions were almost universally business associates. In 1815, for example, Joseph Roy, a white man, went by boat to New Orleans with his free black partners Celestin LeBlanc and Hilaire Marcel LeBlanc to sell chickens at the Crescent City markets (St. Martin Parish, Succession 225).

Though free blacks could openly engage in business with whites and successfully sue them in court, the *gens de couleur libre* could not share a meal or a church pew with whites, even those of inferior economic status. Under the terms of the 1724 code, emancipated blacks were required to show respect to Caucasians, particularly their former owners, and in the early nineteenth century Louisianians institutionalized this time-honored practice (Sterkx 39). In addition, by the end of the Spanish period (1803), free blacks in New Orleans were not permitted to copy the clothing and jewelry of their white neighbors (Gayarré 3:179). As historian H. E. Sterkx has noted:

> Although Louisiana's free Negroes enjoyed exceptional legal and economic privileges, their social status was just above the slave level. At every turn they were victims of social discrimination imposed on them by custom as well as law. . . . In 1806 legislation required free persons of color to pay special respect to White persons. According to a law of that year, they were not allowed to insult or strike Whites under penalties of fine or imprisonment. Free Negroes were not only obligated by this law to speak and answer Whites with respect, but they also were required never "to conceive themselves equal" in any way with persons of the Caucasian race. (240–41)

The institutionalized social isolation of free blacks from the white elite was supplemented by a sporadically enforced legal attempt to isolate the freedmen from the servile population. Fearing collusion between the free black population and slaves in the event of a servile insurrection, whites periodically established, but only haphazardly enforced, legal impediments against social and economic intercourse between members of Louisiana's two lower social orders (Brasseaux 1990:12).

Such artificial barriers between free blacks and slaves, however, were largely unnecessary. All accounts indicate that in the prairie districts, most early free blacks distanced themselves as much, and as quickly, as possible from the horrors of slavery which they themselves had experienced. The course of the group's early development seems to have been charted by matriarchs of the first free black families, who, after separation from their white paramours through either death or abandonment, set about to make themselves and their children economically independent. In some cases, this task was greatly facilitated by a bequest from their departed white benefactors. Others succeeded by dint of their unflagging industry, tenacity, and formidable business acumen (Baker and Kreamer 75–76).

Among the most notable early black Creole matriarchs were Marie Simien and Marie-Jeanne Lemelle of the Opelousas district. Simien, who settled with her four sons in the Opelousas district around 1796, invested her substantial financial resources—evidently derived from her former white paramour—in real estate, developing a vast personal empire by 1818. According to the 1818 tax rolls of St. Landry Parish, Marie Simien owned four parcels of land totaling 7,766 acres. Much of this land, 6,350 acres, consisted of undeveloped prairies and pine forests west of present-day Eunice, which were then considered nearly worthless. Most of the remaining land (1,416 acres), however, was prime farmland in the Bellevue area south of present-day Opelousas, which she cultivated with nine slaves. The uncultivated portion of the estate was used to graze over three hundred head of cattle. Having carved a niche for herself, Simien established an 800-acre plantation for her son George near present-day Eunice (Baker and Kreamer 75–76).

Marie-Jeanne Lemelle, who, along with her two daughters, Jacqueline and Julie (identified as mulatresses), was manumitted at New Orleans on December 5, 1772 (Garic Papers 3:366, Center for Louisiana Studies), followed the precedent established by Marie Simien. Following the manumission, Marie-Jeanne publicly assumed the surname Lemelle. As the mistress of François Lemelle, *fils*, son of a prominent St. Charles Parish planter, she migrated from the New Orleans area to the Opelousas district in the 1780s, approximately ten years after François had established himself in the same area. François Lemelle, *fils*, first appeared in the May 4, 1777, census of the Opelousas district. Marie-Jeanne Lemelle identified François Lemelle, *fils*, as the father of her children in extant baptismal records. To distinguish between François Lemelle, *fils*, and his son François Denis Lemelle, as well as his son François Lemelle by Marie-Jeanne, François Lemelle, *fils* (i.e., Jr.), is sometimes identified as François Lemelle, *père* (i.e., Sr.) in ecclesiastical records. This designation unfortunately leads to confusion between François, *père*, of the Opelousas district, and François, *père*, of St. Charles Parish. To add further to the confusion, his Creole of Color son, François Lemelle, is subsequently called *père* to distinguish himself from his own son, François Lemelle, *fils*. Secondary sources thus understandably contain numerous errors regarding Lemelle's identity. He is described here on the basis of primary source materials, particularly the marriage contract of his natural son Louis (Vidrine and De Ville 49). Marie-Jeanne Lemelle, free woman of color (FWC), is first mentioned in an Opelousas baptismal record dated August 8, 1785. She also appears in the May 1796 census of the Opelousas district (Voorhies 284, 365).

Documents relative to the succession of François Lemelle following his death on September 8, 1789, illustrate the complexity of the relationship between Marie-Jeanne and the Lemelle family. In his last will and testament, François made specific bequests only to his two sons and Marie-Jeanne. He left his sword to Jacques and his gold watch and chain to François Denis. All the household goods, however (beds, mattresses, pillows, bolsters, quilts, blankets, and the like), went not to his daughter but to Marie-Jeanne. In addition to this specific bequest, he bequeathed one-fifth of his estate to Marie-Jeanne "because of the care and pain which the said Marie-Jeanne took of him for many years and for which he had not given her any salary" (Original Acts, Sabatier Collection).

The heirs settled the estate over a four-day period in December 1789 after agreeing to and signing three separate documents. On December 15, 1789, Jean-Baptiste Boutté (acting on behalf of his wife, Marie Louise Lemelle), Jacques, and François Denis consented to all of the terms of their father's last will and testament in favor of Marie-Jeanne, as follows:

> [They] renounce all claims to her servitude, even if the law would have been in their favor. They do so because of the intentions of their deceased mother, Dame Lemelle, whom they remember stating many times that she desired that Marie-Jeanne enjoy freedom. They also do so because of the act of freedom passed by the said François Lemelle stating that he wanted and intended that Marie-Jeanne and all her children, without distinction, enjoy the rights, privileges and prerogatives held by free people (Original Acts, Sabatier Collection).

On December 17, 1789, Marie-Jeanne joined the three legitimate heirs in selling to Martin Duralde, the executor of the estate, an eight-

hundred-arpent tract of land located on the east bank of Bayou Courtableau. The following day, the heirs and Marie-Jeanne estimated the
value of the estate at $3,562.50. Marie-Jeanne accepted as her share the
sum of $712.50, exactly one-fifth of the estimated total value of the es-
tate (Original Acts, Sabatier Collection).

These documents suggest that Marie-Jeanne lived with and cared for
François Lemelle until his death. Both this reference to service and his
children's reference to the wishes of their mother indicate that she had
continued to serve the Lemelle family following François's death. But
following the sale of the plantation to Martin Duralde and the settlement of the estate, Marie-Jeanne moved with her possessions to tracts
of land she had acquired earlier from François Lemelle in transactions
dated November 5, 1784, and July 22, 1786 (Original Acts, St. Landry
Parish Records, Louisiana State Archives and Records Service).

Settling at Isle L'Anglois, east of the present town of Opelousas in
the bend of Bayou Teche near the rural community of Notleyville in
St. Landry Parish, Marie-Jeanne and her three sons set about the task of
improving more than eight hundred acres, much of it acquired from
her former lover. These properties, which included existing buildings
and other improvements, had apparently been partially cleared and
fenced for ranching by Marie-Jeanne's sons before their acquisition from
François Lemelle, who, after the conveyance of land title, received a
portion of the herd's increase as payment for the *vacherie*. François Lemelle also evidently provided Marie-Jeanne with fifteen slaves to assist
his natural sons with the clearing and ranching operations. Once improvements were in place, part of Marie-Jeanne Lemelle's plantation was
parceled out to her sons "to give them status within the community"
(Baker and Kreamer 75–76).

Such direct and substantive involvement in the economic well-being
of children—also characteristic of contemporary Acadian and white
Creole families—was, and would remain throughout the nineteenth
century, a hallmark of Creole of Color society. Contemporary south
Louisiana conveyance records are replete with examples of attempts by
Creoles of Color to establish their children on a sound economic foot-
ing. The example of Zenon Rideau is perhaps the most representative.
A widower formerly married to Héloïse Lavigne, Rideau took as his
second wife Angelic Soileau, but they were not compatible, and in April

1856, Soileau filed an act of separation with a notary, renouncing her claim to any of his property (St. Landry Parish, Miscellaneous Books, 1:313). There is no evidence that she ever filed for or secured a divorce. Rideau then entered a common-law relationship with two sisters, Yacinthe and Lucy Lafleur. Sometime after purchasing from the state public lands at the present site of Palmetto, Louisiana, in 1857, Rideau moved his new family from the Faubourg de Grand Prairie area to the wilderness of east-central St. Landry Parish. In subsequent years, four children were born of Rideau's union with the Lafleur sisters.

Aware that his children by Yacinthe and Lucy had no legal inheritance rights under existing state law, Zenon Rideau executed an act of donation inter vivos by which he transferred to Yacinthe and her child, Mary Magdaline Rideau, and to Lucy Lafleur and her children, Christoval, Joseph, and Colomb Rideau, as well as to two orphan children, Mary and Jules Rideau, a tract of land containing 160 acres at Bayou Petite Prairie with all existing improvements. He also donated a branding iron and twenty-five head of domesticated cattle (Meyers 1–10).

This generous donation, appraised at $3,450, contained numerous safeguards to ensure both Rideau's continued use of the property and provisions for an orderly and safe transfer of the land and cattle.

> 1st The land and improvements herein described and donated to remain in the possession and under the exclusive controll [*sic*] of said Donor with all the revenue derived therefrom during his lifetime and after the death of said Donor, Zenon Rideau, the property herein described to remain in community until the youngest person herein mentioned arrives to the age of twenty-one years.
>
> 2nd That Preval Rideau [one of Zenon's legitimate heirs, who, according to the 1870 census, owned $5,000 in real estate and $300 in personal property] shall be the manager of said plantation & property and guardian of all the said parties herein mentioned who shall still be minors at the death of said Zenon Rideau.
>
> 3rd That after the youngest surviving person herein named arrives at the age of twenty-one years, the property herein described shall be equally divided between all the surviving persons herein mentioned in this donation (St. Landry Parish, Conveyance Book X-1, p. 195).

These provisions of the donation assured that Zenon's concubines and illegitimate children as well as his orphaned grandchildren would receive specified Rideau property despite Louisiana's legal impediments to inheritance. Any donee who preceded Rideau in death, as did Mary Magdalene, was effectively removed from the donation. Had Mary Magdalene had children, they would not have inherited her share of the donation.

Rideau made certain that none of the donees would receive less than twenty acres as their portion of the donation, although they could receive more. The status they acquired as small landowners would have been considerably less than they had enjoyed as part of Zenon's household, but they were nevertheless guaranteed status. And by naming his eldest son, Preval Rideau, as the executor and trustee of the estate, he virtually assured himself that his legitimate heirs would not challenge the donation in probate proceedings. Finally, by maintaining a usufruct to the donated lands, Rideau maintained his own status as a large landholder. Zenon Rideau's wishes were evidently honored by his legal heirs, for the property in question was not included in the 1882 probate of his estate.

At the time of his death, Zenon Rideau still owned three tracts of land, 120 acres valued at $500, 126 acres valued at $1,000, and 120 acres that he had either given or sold to Preval but which Preval collated into the estate, valued at $500. The appraisers of his estate valued the entire estate at $7,054.95, including money loaned to neighbors. The heirs divided the property among themselves and sold the movables at public auction (St. Landry Parish, Probate 4335, Civil District Suit 13596).

Zenon Rideau's deftness at circumventing inheritance restrictions—in a manner reminiscent of the white slave owners who helped establish the region's first free black families—indicates both the degree to which Creoles of Color had become part of the system and the manner in which they were able to use it to their advantage. The extant nineteenth-century records of the civil district courts in St. Landry and St. Martin parishes are replete with suits filed by Creoles of Color to defend their property rights. An analysis of St. Landry Parish civil suits involving Creoles of Color indicates that during the antebellum period, free black plaintiffs enjoyed a remarkable record of success before the local bench, even when the defendants were white. Creoles of Color, for example, won all of their civil suits against white debtors during the period 1800 to 1820, according to the extant Original Acts in the St. Martin Parish Clerk of Court's office. During the antebellum period free persons of color also sporadically filed successful suits to safeguard their beleaguered civil rights.

The consistent courtroom successes of the *gens de couleur libre* in such cases bear ample testimony not only to independence, impartiality, and integrity of the local judiciary but also to the seriousness with which the region's legal profession dealt with challenges to the constitutional rights enjoyed by Louisiana's free black population. In April 1825, for example, the heirs of Pierre Richard brought suit against one Céleste and her children, challenging their status as free persons of color on a technicality. In 1798, Marie, a slave belonging to Pierre Richard, purchased the freedom of her thirteen-month-old daughter, Thestiste, who later assumed the name of Céleste. The Richard heirs maintained that Thestiste and Céleste were different people and that the act of manumission, signed by Pierre Richard, that Céleste produced was not valid. Indeed, the plaintiffs maintained that "neither the said Céleste nor her children, nor any one of them was ever emancipated or made free, nor have they or either of them any claim to freedom on any account whatever." The plaintiffs consequently asked the St. Landry Parish district court to declare Céleste and her family slaves for life; to recognize the Pierre Richard heirs as the "legal owners and proprietors"; to compel the defendants to serve the plaintiffs; and, finally, to provide Céleste with legal counsel (St. Landry Parish, Civil District Suit 970). The district judge summarily rejected the plaintiffs' claim as well as the testimony of Joseph Victor Richard maintaining that Céleste had never been known as Thestiste. In finding for the defendants, the court ruled "that the said Céleste, a free woman of color, and her five [*sic*] children, Jean Louis, Cadet, Sosthene, Vallere, Celestine, and Celisie were and long before the commencement of this suit thence have been officially free and entitled to all the rights to which by the laws of this state free persons of color are entitled." The local jurist concluded his judgment by enjoining the plaintiffs from "disturbing the said Céleste or either of her five [*sic*] children in the enjoyment of their freedom" and by condemning the Richard heirs to pay the court costs totaling $85.80. Failure to comply would result in confiscation of Richard property, but slaves owned by the Richards were specifically exempted from the confiscation order (St. Landry Parish, Civil District Suit 970).

In a similar case, tried in 1830 and 1831, Mary Anne Marchand brought suit against the persons appointed by the court to administer the probate proceedings by which the plaintiff and her children were to be emancipated. Mary Anne, who inherited considerable real and movable property from her deceased former master, François Marchand, first brought suit against Jean M. Debaillon, executor of the Marchand estate. Filed on April 21, 1830, this suit successfully blocked Debaillon's attempted sale of town lots and buildings in Opelousas and Washington bequeathed to Mary Anne by the François Marchand estate. The second suit was brought by Mary Anne Marchand against her court-appointed curator, Benjamin F. Linton, whom she accused of unnecessarily delaying her emancipation proceedings. Unwilling to pursue the matter, Linton tendered his resignation on January 2, 1832, and later the same day, Judge George King signed an order appointing Jean M. Debaillon, Mary Anne's surprising nominee as Linton's replacement, as the plaintiff's new curator (St. Landry Parish, Probate Court Suits 70, 100).

Free women of color were equally willing to confront public officials whenever their legal and civil rights were challenged, as demonstrated by one case heard by the St. Landry district court. On May 16, 1829, Harriet Scott appeared before the bench to request restoration of her freedom. Scott claimed to have been born a free woman in Providence, Rhode Island, and to have migrated at an unspecified date to Marietta, Ohio. Sometime later she went to Kentucky, where she was mistaken for a slave and "sold as such." Scott then legally challenged her enslavement, but before her suit could be brought to trial, two unscrupulous slave dealers whisked her off to the New Orleans slave markets. While in the Crescent City, Scott escaped and traveled to Washington, Louisiana, aboard the steamboat *Integrity.* "Upon some proceedings instigated by the Capt[.] of the said boat she was committed to the prison of the said Parish [of St. Landry]." The detainee, acting through attorney Benjamin Linton, requested a writ of habeas corpus as well as a judgment of $350 against Sheriff George Jackson of St. Landry Parish as punitive damages for false imprisonment. Confronted with the prospect of a personal lawsuit, Jackson assigned blame for Scott's detention to local Justice of the Peace Edward Taylor and petitioned the bench for dismissal of the charges against him. Judge Seth Lewis dismissed the charges against Jackson but released Scott on bail pending a full hearing on her legal status (St. Landry Parish, Civil District Suit 1514).

Free man of color Zenon Rideau also used personal lawsuits against officeholders as a means of forcing recalcitrant public officials to accede to his untimely request to emancipate one of his slaves. As the slavery issue became increasingly politically and emotionally charged in the late antebellum period, manumission of slaves became correspondingly more difficult as legal and extralegal impediments were placed in the path of slave owners seeking to liberate their human chattel. Such slave owners, for example, were required to post bonds securing funds for the care of aged former slaves, thus ensuring that emancipated bondsmen would not eventually become wards of the state. Such bonds were easily procured by affluent free persons of color, but the intractability of increasingly unsympathetic public officials charged with the responsibility of approving manumissions was less easily overcome. Obviously exasperated with hostile local public officials, Zenon Rideau filed suit against District Attorney William Mouton in an effort to force a decision regarding his petition to free Aimé(e), an eighteen-year-old slave who had become the common-law wife of Rideau's son Jean-Baptiste Rideau. Because Aimé(e) was pregnant, and because, under Louisiana law, children derived their legal status from that of their mother, Zenon Rideau was compelled to act precipitously. Mouton chose not to challenge Rideau's suit, and, on March 1, 1856, the plaintiff won the case by default. On June 4, 1856, Zenon Rideau filed with Louisiana's governor a $2,000 bond as security for Aimé(e) and Zelin, her three-week-old child (St. Landry Parish, Civil District Suit 7646). Rideau again challenged the local establishment in 1881, this time unsuccessfully. On October 20, 1881, Rideau sought an injunction to prevent St. Landry Parish Sheriff C. C. Duson from confiscating two mules. The suit was dismissed, and the plaintiff was ordered to pay all court costs (St. Landry Parish, Civil District Suit 13142).

Creoles of Color effectively used the local legal system to protect their interests until well after the Civil War, despite concerted efforts by whites to deny them their rights. As white resentment of Creoles of Color mounted in the late antebellum period, particularly in the turbulent 1850s, white creditors sued their Creole of Color debtors for indebtedness more and more frequently, evidently as part of a concerted effort to coerce the *gens de couleur libre* into leaving the prairie region. Such legal intimidation, however, proved unsuccessful, and during the height of the effort to eradicate the free black population of the Attakapas and Opelousas areas, Creoles of Color won 80 percent of all suits for indebtedness against them in St. Landry Parish.

Even during the Civil War, Creoles of Color won more civil suits than they lost, though the gap between success and failure closed significantly. The Creoles' declining success rate, however, was clearly a result of their falling economic fortunes and not of changing racial biases on the part of the district bench. The best example is the wartime suits filed by Auguste Donato, *fils,* who sought and secured an injunction against Gustave E. Louallier. After filing a $2,000 bond against wrongful or unjustified litigation and producing proof of his active support of the Confederacy, Auguste Donato, *fils,* submitted the following petition to the district court:

> The petition of Auguste Donato, *fils* a free man of color of the parish of St. Landry, state of Louisiana, with respect represents that he is in the service of the Confederate States under the provisions of the act of the Congress of said Confederate States, approved the 17th February 1864 entitled an act to further increase the efficiency of the army by the employment of free negroes and slaves in certain capacities.
>
> That he was a planter in this parish residing near Opelousas up to the month of April 1863, when the public enemy of the Confederate States [i.e., the Union army] destroyed all his fencing and carried away most of his field hands.
>
> That he produced cotton in 1861 and 1862 which is yet unsold, and which he removed to a distant portion of the parish to prevent its fall in the hands of the enemy, and in obedience to orders from the military authorities of the Confederate States.
>
> That on the 23d instant without any consent of your petitioner and without any notification to him one Gustave E. Louaillier [*sic*] of the said parish of St. Landry, proceeded to the house of one Evariste Guillory free man of color distant about twelve miles from Opelousas in this parish, and forcibly took possession of fifteen bales of cotton, the property of your petitioner, without any process of law and without any right to do so, and without making any compensation therefor to your petitioner.
>
> That he carried fifteen bales of cotton away to parts unknown to your petitioner. That he has caused damages to your petitioner by his illegal acts to the amount of four thousand five hundred dollars ($4500), the value of said fifteen bales of cotton, besides the further damages of five hundred dollars fees of counsel which your petitioner has been obliged

to incur to prosecute this suit to final judgement. That said Louallier proceeding illegally and wrongfully, and with force of arms, is about taking other cotton belonging to your petitioner saved at the house of said Evariste Guillory free man of color and also some cotton saved at the houses of Donato Guillory and of Casimir Guillory free man of color, in this parish of St. Landry about twelve miles from Opelousas.

That said Louaillier will remove said cotton beyond the jurisdiction of your honorable Court and do an irreparable wrong to your petitioner, unless prohibited to take said cotton from said places and to remove the same therefrom. (St. Landry Parish, Civil District Suit 9454)

In summary, the suit requested the sum of $5,000, plus an injunction against Louallier to prohibit him from taking additional cotton. The petition was followed by an oath indicating that since January 18, 1861, Auguste Donato had not taken any oath to support the government or Constitution of the United States and that he had not had any dealing with agents of the United States government. He further abjured that the facts as stated in his petition were true and that therefore the injunction was necessary.

Donato produced as proof of his allegations the certificate of impressment issued by Theo. D. Miller and filed by Gustave Louallier, agents of the Confederate States government, and presented to P. D. Hardy, Donato's attorney and agent, for fifteen bales of cotton seized at the plaintiff's Bois Mallet farm:

> I certify that by virtue of authority from Genl E. Kirby-Smith, I have impressed this 23d day of December at Evariste Guillory's [residence,] Mallet Woods, Parish of St. Landry, State of Louisiana, the following property, viz. Fifteen bales of cotton, that the same could not be otherwise procured and was taken thro [sic] absolute necessity: I further certify that the said A. Donato fils not having taken the oath to secure him a local appraisement, is entitled to payment at the schedule rates established by the Board of Commissioners, to wit forty cents per pound making the aggregate sum of Twenty-five hundred and seventy one & 20/100 dollars. [signed] Theo D. Miller, Agent C.S. Govt. (St. Landry Parish, Civil District Suit 9454)

Citing his authorization to seize the disputed cotton as well as the state's "schedule rate" of forty cents per pound set out in the certificate, which, he maintained, entitled the plaintiff to only $2,571.20, Louallier countered that Donato had only to go to the proper Confederate authorities to secure the payment authorized by the certificate. Louallier also informed the court that he had offered the certificate to Evariste Guillory, who had refused it. The Confederate agent then went to the residence of Auguste Donato, *fils,* but found him absent, so he gave the certificate to P. D. Hardy, the plaintiff's agent and attorney at the time. Despite the veracity of Louallier's assertions, the court granted the injunction on the date filed, December 28, 1864, pending adjudication of the claim scheduled for the fourth Monday in April 1865.

The outcome of the dispute is veiled in mystery. No extant court documents indicate whether Donato secured $5,000 or even whether he agreed to the $2,571.20 the certificate offered. The question is moot in any event for, given the late date of the trial, it is doubtful that Donato would ever have spent the disputed Confederate money had he received a favorable judgment. But a favorable judgment had never been Donato's principal objective; he had successfully used the system to achieve his unstated goal of preventing the confiscation of any more cotton.

The collective legal fortunes of the prairie Creoles of Color waned during the Reconstruction and post-Reconstruction eras as a result of their increasingly precarious economic circumstances. Devastated by the ravages of war and its aftermath, Creoles of Color, like their crestfallen white counterparts, increasingly fell prey to creditors collecting overdue debts (Tables 5 and 6). Yet the former free people of color con-

TABLE 5

Civil Cases Involving Creoles of Color for Indebtedness
in St. Landry Parish, 1855–1900

Dates	Plaintiff	Percent	Defendant	Percent
1855–1861	4	40	6	60
1861–1865	2	40	3	60
1866–1877	5	29	12	71
1878–1900	1	07	13	93

Source: St. Landry Parish, Civil District Suits, 1855–1900.

TABLE 6

Percentage of Civil Suits for Indebtedness Won by
Creoles of Color in St. Landry Parish, 1855–1900

Dates	Won	Percent	Lost	Percent
1855–1861	8	80	2	20
1861–1865	3	60	2	40
1866–1877	4	24	13	76
1878–1900	5	36	9	64

Source: St. Landry Parish, Civil District Suits, 1855–1900.

tinued to use the legal system to their advantage whenever possible, as is demonstrated by the following chain of transactions. In 1866, former FPC Auguste Donato, *fils,* brought suit against Jean Pierre Close's estate for collection of an overdue debt (St. Landry Parish, Civil District Suit 9657). On April 12, 1866, Gustave Donato bought land measuring six arpents frontage by sixty-five arpents depth, part of the Vieux Vacherie near present-day Notleyville, from the Close estate at a sheriff's sale (St. Landry Parish, Conveyance Book U-1, p. 103). Three days later, Gustave Donato sold the property to Julien Bordelon of Rider's Bridge (St. Landry Parish, Conveyance Book U-1, p. 107). In May 1870, Auguste Donato bought the same tract of land at a sheriff's sale of Julien Bordelon's property. Donato, who had just returned to St. Landry Parish after a five-year residence in New Orleans, then leased the property to Bordelon, thereby reducing the former white yeoman to tenantry (St. Landry Parish, Miscellaneous Book 4, p. 375). On February 5, 1871, Auguste Donato, *fils,* sold the Vieux Vacherie tract to Joseph Estorge (St. Landry Parish, Conveyance Book Y-1, p. 248). Thus, within a five-year period, the Donato family thrice benefited from the repeated sale of a single piece of property, while also enjoying the proceeds of an annual lease.

Women in the Creole of Color community proved equally adept at using the legal system to their advantage. Louisiana's civil laws, derived from Roman antecedents, provided the Pelican State's female property holders not only greater protection of individual property rights but also far greater opportunities to manage property and engage in business without interference from their husbands than did any common-law system. Women retained exclusive control over any property not brought into the marital community of acquets and gains, including both property owned at the time of the wedding as well as property inherited after a union was forged.

Existing legal mechanisms, based on the "Sixty-first Law of Torro as well as provisions contained in the ninth title, third book, fifth of the recopilation de Castillo," put teeth into women's property rights (St. Landry Parish, Conveyance Book E-1, p. 218). Before marriage, prospective grooms posted a bond—$500 in the 1830s and early 1840s and $300 in the 1850s—to secure a marriage license. St. Landry Parish courthouse records indicate that the practice of acquiring marriage bonds persisted in the prairie region until at least 1948. As the marriage bonds of Michel Comeau, FMC, and Victorin Ledée, FWC, November 19, 1839 (A-588); David Guillory, FMC, to Caroline Papillon, FWC, September 13, 1842 (No. 67); and Eli Lucullus, FMC, and Angèle B. Fontenot, FWC, July 21, 1851 (No. 856 1/2) clearly attest, whenever the groom or his father was unable to raise the necessary money, other relatives stepped forward as guarantors for the bonds. The bond was intended to protect the separate property of the bride as well as any community property the couple might acquire. The bond also effectively created a tacit mortgage on all community property. Property sold by either spouse required the written approval of the other spouse; otherwise, title to the property would remain forever clouded. The documentary record indicates that Creole women jealously guarded and fully exercised their property rights, both over their individual property and within the marital community.

The business acumen of female property holders is reflected in scores of business transactions involving myriad forms of property. In every instance, these women demonstrated not only that they were cognizant of their property and individual rights but also that they were fully capable of using the system to protect those rights and achieve their goals. Free women of color bought and sold land, slaves, and other property. Indeed, the conveyance records in the St. Martin Parish Clerk of Court's Office document twenty such transactions involving free black women between November 1810 and May 1814. Sometimes these transfers included property received earlier from their white benefactors, as in the case of Marie-Josèphe, who, on December 14, 1811, sold to Pierre Broussard four hundred superficial arpents of land given to her by Joseph Prévost (St. Martin Parish, Original Acts, 26:242). In most instances, however, these women disposed of property that they themselves had acquired.

Free women of color also manumitted slaves (St. Martin Parish, Original Acts, 27:92, 28:8) and provided for the orderly transfer of property to their heirs. On November 2, 1807, for instance, Filnotion, a free woman of color recently manumitted by André Claude Boutté, registered her will providing for the orderly transfer of her property to her five children (St. Martin Parish, Original Acts, 23:151).

Women in the free black community also ran farms, plantations, and, in the case of Marie Louise Lemelle, mercantile businesses (St. Landry Parish, Civil District Suit 11013). They also sued debtors, initiated interdiction proceedings against incapacitated relatives (St. Landry Parish, Probate Court Suit 121), brought suit against husbands as a means of protecting their paraphernal property rights (St. Landry Parish, Civil District Suit 1013), and blocked unfounded interdiction efforts against themselves.

In one notable case of foiled interdiction, Julien Lartigue indicated that his daughter was mentally and physically incapacitated, and he asked the district court to appoint him her curator. The judge scheduled a hearing and appointed prominent local politician Caleb L. Swayze to represent the Lartigue girl. Swayze, after meeting with Angeline Lartigue, filed a countersuit against Julien Lartigue, maintaining that the plaintiff was incapable of seeking the requested curatorship because he was not her father as he had claimed. In addition, Swayze insisted that the defendant was sound of mind and body and capable of managing her own affairs. The judge's disposition in this case has been lost. The absence of a judgment raises several important questions: Was Julien Lartigue attempting to gain control over Angeline Lartigue's property for his own benefit? Did the court attempt to protect Angeline's interests by appointing a disinterested third party to represent her? Or, by denying Julien Lartigue's claim of paternity, was an unscrupulous attorney attempting to take control of her affairs himself and take advantage of Angeline's alleged incapacitation? Swayze's lofty economic status and the decision to appoint legal counsel for the defendant, however, suggest that Angeline Lartigue may well have been spared the malicious designs of a covetous relative (St. Landry Parish, Civil District Suit 9364).

Free women of color were remarkably like white female property holders in their determination to protect their material interests at all costs, for, under the civil code, property provided Louisiana women a degree of independence unknown in the rest of the antebellum South. Yet they differed significantly from their white Catholic counterparts in their greater willingness to leave doomed marriages at a time when divorces were virtually unknown in Catholic south Louisiana. Indeed, husbands of estranged wives initiated all of the seven suits for separation, divorce, and custody of children involving Creoles of Color in St. Landry Parish between 1855 and 1900 (St. Landry Parish, Civil District Suits 8950, 9408, 9882, 11029, 12298, 14557, 15695).

The careers of Manon Baldwin and Marie Louise Lemelle—respectively members of new and old black Creole families—offer perhaps the best insight into the life experiences of ambitious and independent women in the Creole of Color community. Marie Louise Lemelle secured a judgment of separation of paraphernal property from her husband, Joseph Delmont Donato, on January 7, 1869 (St. Landry Parish, Civil District Suit 11013). The 1870 census identifies Lemelle's husband as a grocer with property valued at $1,600; courthouse records indicate that Marie Louise Lemelle was also a grocer who maintained her individual property separate from the marital community. Lemelle used the proceeds of her grocery business to engage in land speculation. On November 8, 1871, for example, she purchased a 100.5-by-169.5-foot lot on the corner of North and Court streets in Opelousas from Auguste Donato. Lemelle paid $2,000 for the property. On November 29, 1871, she sold a lot for $150 in Church Addition to Washington Gails. Then, on December 5, 1872, she purchased as her separate property a 62.7-acre tract of land from Céleste Lastrapes, the widow of Rice Garland, for $1,522.46. She subsequently retired and leased her store first to Sam Levy in 1887 and then to Clement and Wilson in 1888 (St. Landry Parish, Conveyance Book Z-1, pp. 1, 45, 598).

Although many free people of color in the prairie parishes, like the Lemelles, derived their wealth and power through intermarriage and the extension of family alliances and property holdings, some were not so fortunate as to be born or to marry into the more prominent families.

These individuals had to depend on their wits and resources to accumulate wealth, power, or both. Manon Baldwin, a free woman of color in the community of Opelousas, never learned to read or write, but fifty documents or sets of documents concerning her business and legal activities exist in the records of the clerk of court for St. Landry Parish.

Manon Baldwin first appears in the records as a thirty-year-old mulatto slave woman with a four-year-old child. Although she was the property of Etienne de la Morandière, *fils,* she and her son were living with Isaac Baldwin, an Opelousas attorney. On March 7, 1808, De la Morandière agreed to sell Manon to Baldwin for $800. Because Baldwin had only $550 in cash, they agreed that the remaining $250 would be due on May 1, 1809, and that Manon would remain mortgaged until payment was made. The sale document also indicates that Baldwin relinquished any claim that he might have to the right of purchasing Jean-Baptiste, the infant child of Manon (St. Landry Parish, Conveyance Book A-1, p. 248). This document unfortunately does not clarify the relationship between Baldwin and Jean-Baptiste, but one can only assume that De la Morandière and Baldwin had earlier agreed to some

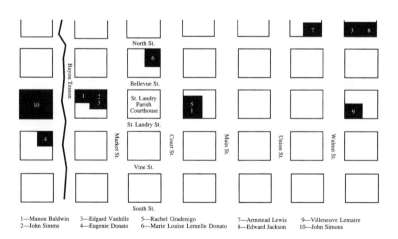

| 1—Manon Baldwin | 3—Edgard Vanhille | 5—Rachel Gradenigo | 7—Armstead Lewis | 9—Villeneuve Lemaire |
| 2—John Simms | 4—Eugenie Donato | 6—Marie Louise Lemelle Donato | 8—Edward Jackson | 10—John Simons |

Free Person of Color/Creole of Color Properties
Opelousas, 1837-1871

sort of right of purchase. Apparently Baldwin made a timely payment because on June 14, 1809, he executed a document emancipating Manon. Manon signed the document with an "x" (St. Landry Parish, Conveyance Book B-1, pp. 136–37).

After her emancipation, in her first legal transaction, dated June 10, 1812, Manon exchanged with De la Morandière a young female slave named Sophie for her son Jean-Baptiste (sometimes called simply Baptiste). Although the document fails to identify Sophie and to indicate how she came into Manon's possession, Isaac Baldwin signed the document as security for Manon's ownership of Sophie and promised to defend De la Morandière's title to Sophie against all claims (St. Landry Parish, Conveyance Book B-1, p. 321).

As a result of this transaction, Manon owned her quadroon son, but under the Louisiana slave code, she was unable to emancipate him until his twenty-first birthday. Consequently, less than one month after this act of exchange, eight-year-old Jean-Baptiste, with the consent of his mother, signed indenture papers with Isaac Baldwin for a period of twelve years and six months. Yet because it was drafted as an ostensibly legal transaction between Jean-Baptiste and Baldwin, this document treated Jean-Baptiste as though he were already free and able to execute a document in his own behalf. It also provided the young apprentice with a legal guardian and protector until his twenty-first birthday (St. Landry Parish, Conveyance Book B-1, p. 343).

Manon continued her alliance with Baldwin until 1815, when he decided to close his law practice in Opelousas and move to Rapides Parish. Manon apparently chose to end their relationship at that point. Baldwin thereupon sold to her, for $500, the lot measuring 50 feet (frontage) by 169 feet (depth) and a building in which they had resided and he had maintained his law office. The property was located directly across from Opelousas's courthouse square on what is now the northeast corner of the intersection of Landry and Court streets, currently serving as the law offices of Domengeaux and Wright (St. Landry Parish, Conveyance Book C-1, p. 163). On this location Manon (using the name Manon Baldwin, although she and Isaac could not, and had not, married legally) promptly established herself as a prominent businesswoman in Opelousas. In addition to serving as her residence, the property was also a boardinghouse, restaurant, and tavern. Her proximity to the courthouse square, her relationship as provider of goods and services to lawyers, judges, jailers, prisoners, and the general public who frequented the courthouse, as well as her experience with the workings of the legal system during her alliance with Baldwin, apparently became her source of power and security during the remainder of her life (St. Landry Parish, Conveyance Book G-1, p. 55).

Manon understood that the ownership of property, both real and chattel, provided a person with status and security. She also understood that the closer the property was to the seat of power in the parish, the more power she could call upon when necessary. Between 1816 and 1838, she purchased at least three other properties within a block of the courthouse square. At a public auction on July 26, 1816, Manon entered the high bid of $255 for a lot described as having twenty-five English feet front by forty-five English feet depth, bounded on the south by Robert Taylor, north by Joseph Reeves, and west by the public square.

The two pieces of property owned by Manon were separated by the lot of Robert Taylor (St. Landry Parish, Estate 81). Sometime between 1820 and 1836, Manon acquired a second tract on which she built two houses, one to serve as her residence and the second for persons she employed. The property was located next to the Market House on the public square and faced Bellevue Street with Bayou Rouge as its western boundary (St. Landry Parish, Conveyance Book N-1, pp. 390–91). Baldwin purchased the third property, a town lot on Bellevue Street, immediately west of Bayou Rouge and therefore adjacent to her second tract, from Joel Bell on April 30, 1838 (St. Landry Parish, Mortgage Book 2, p. 82).

On July 11, 1825, Manon Baldwin and Michael Derringher bought from Augustin, a Native American, property described as having three and one-half arpents frontage on each side of Bayou Rouge by the ordinary depth (i.e., forty arpents). The sale was made in consideration for services rendered by Manon and Derringher during Augustin's imprisonment (St. Landry Parish, Conveyance Book G-1, p. 55). Manon also acquired a fractional lot in the town of Washington (St. Landry Parish, Estate 81).

Manon's acquisitions were not restricted to real estate. In addition to Jean-Baptiste, she purchased at least five other slaves. When she was financially strapped, she treated her slaves as investments; at other times it appeared that she made the purchases for humanitarian reasons. For example, when she needed help in running the boardinghouse, she purchased a thirty-three- or thirty-four-year-old slave woman variously known as Harriet, Harriette, and Henriette (St. Landry Parish, Conveyance Book C-1, pp. 421–22). Economic reverses in 1819 forced Baldwin to borrow $900 from Opelousas attorney Joseph Andrus. As security for the loan she mortgaged her income-producing property on the courthouse square (St. Landry Parish, Conveyance Book E-1, p. 177). To raise the money needed to repay Andrus, she sold Henriette to a free Negro named Joseph Carrière for $850.

Andrus lifted the mortgage he held against Henriette, thereby allowing Manon to sell her to Carrière. Under the terms of the agreement, Carrière made an initial down payment of $250, followed by installments of $250 in March 1820 and $350 in March 1821 (St. Landry Parish, Conveyance Book A-1, p. 43).

This transaction may have served both economic and humanitarian purposes. In his last will and testament, dated June 16, 1820 (St. Landry Parish, Probate 292), Joseph Carrière acknowledged that he still owed Manon $350 for Henriette. He ordered this debt paid and further ordered that Henriette be emancipated as soon as possible after his death (St. Landry Parish, Notary Book A, p. 190). Henriette may have been Carrière's wife or concubine, but if so, one would assume that he would have given her more than her freedom. In his last will and testament, however, he bequeathed all his cattle to his niece Marie Joseph Louais. All debts owed to him had already been converted to Manon's possession in partial payment of Henriette. All that remained was an old horse that died before it could be sold. John Moore certified that "the balance of the debt due by the deceased at his death to Manon for the purchase of the negro woman Harriett has been paid out of the said Harriett's own money in order that she might obtain her liberty—which liberty has been given as requested by the deceased in his said last Will and Testament." One might speculate that Henriette continued to work for Manon after her sale to Carrière and that she had frugally saved her money with the intention of buying her freedom. She obviously knew how sick Carrière was when his last will and testament was prepared in 1820. She also knew that she was still mortgaged to Manon until the last $350 was paid. Carrière, knowing that he was dying, might also have given her sufficient money to complete the payment to Manon.

In the interim, Manon's debt to Andrus fell due; she was unable to pay, and Andrus secured a judgment against her. The judge ordered the property seized and sold (St. Landry Parish, Civil District Suit 488). Manon apparently convinced Andrus not to foreclose on the mortgage and allow her more time to acquire the money to repay the loan. In January 1821, she arranged the indenture of her son Jean-Baptiste Montgomery to Benjamin Lewis for a term of three years for the sum of $100. In the indenture agreement, Jean-Baptiste is described as a free boy of color about the age of sixteen. Jean-Baptiste signed the indentures with the consent of his mother, Manon Baldwin. No reference is made to the fact that he was at least theoretically still indentured to Isaac Baldwin. The use of the name Montgomery in this document indicates that he was not Isaac Baldwin's son (St. Landry Parish, Conveyance Book E-1, pp. 412–13).

On April 30, 1821, Manon secured a judgment against John Moore, testamentary executor of Joseph Carrière's estate, for $350 with 10 percent interest from January 20, 1820. Payment, however, was not immediately forthcoming. Not until December 22, 1822, did Manon acknowledge receipt from John Moore of full payment of the remaining debt. Baldwin then rescinded the mortgage for which Henriette had stood as security (St. Landry Parish, Civil District Suit 516).

Thwarted in her efforts to secure sufficient funds to satisfy Andrus and in a last-ditch effort to save her income-producing property, Manon turned to the only economic asset she still possessed, her son Jean-Baptiste. On September 17, 1822, she sold Jean-Baptiste, "quadroon slave for life," whom she had originally acquired from Etienne de la Morandière, *fils,* to Gerard Chrétien for $650 (St. Landry Parish, Notary Book B, pp. 369–70). The bill of sale was duly passed before Judge George King, who certified that there were no mortgages or liens on a mulatto boy slave named Baptiste but negligently overlooked the fact that Baptiste's indenture to Benjamin Lewis had not yet expired. When it became apparent that Chrétien intended to use the young man as a field hand, Manon moved quickly to regain control over her son. On October 4, 1822, she negotiated a rental agreement whereby she would pay Chrétien $100 per year for seven years (St. Landry Parish, Conveyance Book B-1, p. 375). It thereupon became apparent to Andrus that Manon would not be able to meet her obligation to him, and on April 4, 1823, he allowed the sheriff to seize and sell the property he purchased for the value of the judgment (St. Landry Parish, Sheriff Book A, pp. 118–19). He then became Manon's landlord; she continued to occupy the premises and conduct business as usual. Andrus remained her landlord until October 5, 1833, when he and Manon executed an act of exchange in which she transferred to him her share of the three-and-one-half by forty-two-arpent tract near Bayou Rouge in exchange for ownership of the lot on market square which he had acquired at the sheriff's sale. An interesting condition of the exchange was that Manon acquired ownership of the property only during her lifetime with title to revert to Andrus or his heirs or assigns upon her death (St. Landry Parish, Conveyance Book K-1, p. 429).

Relieved of the pressure of the debt to Andrus, Manon began husbanding her resources to rectify her questionable actions toward Jean-Baptiste. On August 24, 1824, she and Chrétien entered into an agreement setting aside the earlier rental agreement and converting it to a sale. Manon agreed to pay $1,200 in equal installments of $300 beginning on the second anniversary of the sale, with payments to be made in the second, third, fourth, and fifth years. Jean-Baptiste would remain mortgaged to Chrétien until final payment was made (St. Landry Parish, Conveyance Book C-1, p. 27). This is the last reference to Jean-Baptiste that could be located. It is quite possible that he died sometime between 1824 and 1833, which would explain why Manon agreed to the conditions of the act of exchange between herself and Andrus in 1833.

One additional slave sale gives some insight into Manon's personality. In 1839, when Manon was over sixty years of age, she paid Gabriel Lyons $250 for a three- or four-year-old-orphan slave girl named Eliza (St. Landry Parish, Labyche Notarial Acts 014595). The following condition stipulated in the conveyance sheds considerable light:

> It being however well understood, that a part of the consideration for which the sale and conveyance is made is that the said Manon Baldwin is to emancipate the said mulatto girl slave when she arrives at the full age of majority, or before that period if the law permits it, and the said Manon Baldwin hereby promises to obligate herself, her heirs, executors and administrators to pass an act of emancipation in favor of the said orphan Eliza at the shortest period that the same can be done by law, giving her, the said orphan Eliza, all the prerogatives and privileges of other free persons or as though she had been born free.

(The final statement of this conveyance mimicked the language of the Code Noir promulgated by Governor Jean-Baptiste Le Moyne de Bienville in 1724.) Although the document provides no clues as to Manon's motivation in executing this conveyance, one must assume that she made this purchase for humanitarian reasons. Manon came into possession of at least six slaves during the course of her life. Although no additional slave sales by Manon or acts of emancipation were located, no slaves were listed in the inventory of her estate. The only reference to slaves in her last will and testament was her stated desire that her bedding and body linen be given to those slaves who attended her during her last moments of life.

Manon Baldwin's business activities were not necessarily unusual. What was unusual was her willingness to use the court system to protect her rights. In an era when most men and women, whether Caucasian or free people of color, tried to avoid court action, Manon had no hesitancy about filing suit to ensure that her rights were not violated. In May 1817, Manon sold to Michael Beck a twenty-five-foot by forty-five-foot lot on the courthouse square on condition that Beck would pay $100 in one year and $150 in the second year for a total sale price of $250. When Beck defaulted on his payments, Manon filed suit in the July term of the court in 1819. She fell victim to Louisiana's unusual court system, which conducted trials in both English and French. When the English-speaking attorney spoke, those members of the jury who spoke only French left the jury box and joined the audience. When the French-speaking attorney spoke, those members of the jury who spoke only English left the jury box and joined the audience. Therefore, it was possible for a jury to decide on a case with virtually none of the evidence clearly understood. Such was the case with Manon's first foray into the arena of the court system. The jury, totally misunderstanding the particulars of the case, awarded Beck judgment for $250 (St. Landry Parish, Conveyance Book D-1, pp. 31–32). Undaunted by this setback, Manon immediately filed an appeal and indicated that the judgment was based on manifest error. She posted bond for the $250 judgment that the original trial court had awarded to Beck. After reviewing the particulars in the case, the judge granted her appeal and a new trial was held in November 1819 (St. Landry Parish, Civil District Suit 413).

One would think that after such a near disastrous turn of events Manon would be hesitant to seek court action for redress of grievances in the future. In September 1821, however, she filed suit against one Joseph Irwin, charging that Irwin had broken into her home on the evening of September 22, 1821, brandishing a naked dagger and threating her and her assembled guests. She further charged that he beat her and physically and verbally abused her. In her plea she requested judgment against Irwin and damages of $500. In his response to the charges, Irwin insisted that Manon was conducting an illegal assembly of free people of color and slaves and that he merely went to her place to look for a runaway slave. He claimed that any injury Manon suffered was her own fault because of her refusal to show him a permit for the gathering. One of the documents produced in court, however, was a permit issued on September 21, 1822, allowing Manon Baldwin to conduct a ball for free people of color. The permit stipulated that slaves were to be admitted to the ball only if they had a permit from their masters. After reviewing the evidence, a jury of twelve landowners found Irwin guilty of the alleged trespass and ordered him to pay damages to Manon of $25. The court records include a receipt from Manon to Joseph Irwin indicating that he paid her the $25 judgment (St. Landry Parish, Civil District Suit 554).

Despite her apparent familiarity with the law and the workings of the legal system, Manon ran afoul of the system in a suit filed against her by Thomas Alexander. He had in his possession a note signed by Manon Baldwin with her ordinary mark for $500, dated July 28, 1819, payable on January 31, 1820, to A. Alexander. Although numerous demands had been made for payment, Manon had always refused to pay. Thomas Alexander, as curator of the vacant estate of A. Alexander, requested that the court order Manon to say under oath whether she did or did not sign by affixing her ordinary mark on the note. Manon contended that although she did indeed sign her "x" to the note, it was not properly witnessed, nor was it ever intended to be collected because she never received either directly or indirectly any legal valuable or good consideration. Upon her admission that she had signed the note, the jury found for the plaintiff, Thomas Alexander. Because the jury was not allowed to hear the particulars in the case, Manon filed an appeal and was granted a new trial.

The new trial was heard at the May session of the court in 1826. The foreman of the jury was Etienne de la Morandière, *fils,* Manon's former owner. The interrogatories, responses, and counterinterrogatories and responses for the second trial provided the judge, but not the jury, with all the particulars. In her response to the interrogatories from Thomas

Alexander, Manon indicated that she had lived for a period of time during the year 1819 in New Orleans with A. Alexander, "rendering him divers important services in family economy." She indicated that as recompense for these services Alexander gave her a Negro woman slave named Lilly. In the conveyance transferring Lilly, Alexander had indicated that the consideration was for a certain amount of money to purchase Lilly. Manon, however, testified that no money ever changed hands. Because Alexander feared that his heirs would recognize the transaction as an illegal donation, he requested that Manon sign a note in hand for the sum of $500. He assured her that the note would not be valid, that no attempt would be made to collect it, and furthermore, that it could never be collected because there were no legal witnesses. (Apparently, Alexander intended to mark the note paid at some later date. Unfortunately for Manon, he died, leaving an apparently valid note.) The note was intended to confound his heirs. She swore that no witness was present and that the person named as witness was unknown to her. She further contended that the name of the witness was actually written by A. Alexander "in his own hand." She therefore requested that the court have Thomas Alexander prove that such a witness existed, that he was actually present, and that he indeed signed as witness to the note. Only these facts could prove the legality of the note. In his response to her interrogatories, Thomas Alexander requested that all testimony except the admission that she signed the document be stricken from Manon's responses. His request to the court was based on his assertion that her interrogatories and responses to his were scandalous, libelous, and impertinent. He further contended that they contained matter that, if true, proved collusion between A. Alexander and Manon to defraud the Alexander heirs. Furthermore, because Manon acknowledged signing the note, it was immaterial whether it was properly witnessed. In the final analysis, the judge accepted Thomas Alexander's assertion that Manon could not use, in her defense, proof that she was party to fraud and collusion in the commission of a crime. Since Manon, as a free woman of color, could not testify in open court, the jury could act only on the fact that she acknowledged having signed the note. Given these conditions, the jury again rendered judgment for the plaintiff and ordered Manon to pay the $500 (St. Landry Parish, Civil District Suit 974).

Manon again attempted to appeal. Judge Seth Lewis carefully collected all the papers in the case for presentation to a higher court, but there is no evidence that the Louisiana Supreme Court ever heard or acted on the appeal (*Louisiana Reports Books, Martin Reports,* (N.S.) Vol. 5). It would thus appear that Manon Baldwin became the only victim of a scheme her lover had concocted to fool his heirs.

In spite of this setback, Manon was not deterred in her determination to pursue her rights in court whenever this was the only way to secure what was rightfully hers, regardless of how small the sum. On June 4, 1830, Manon submitted to the executor of the estate of François Marchand, one Jean Marie Debaillon, a bill of particulars for goods provided and services rendered at the funeral of Marchand. The probate of the estate was apparently taking too long to satisfy her, and she filed suit and won a judgment of $32.12 1/2 against the executor of the estate (St. Landry Parish, Probate Court 99).

Manon never married and apparently had only one son, Jean-Baptiste. Although she formed liaisons with Isaac Baldwin and later with A. Alexander, her experience with the latter must have convinced her that she must rely on her own devices for personal and economic security. For example, she procured the assistance of slaves and indentured servants in running her establishment. Eugenie Roussillon, a fifteen-year-old free person of color, was one of the girls who entered Manon's service. With the consent of her mother, Rosalie Malveau, Roussillon apprenticed herself to Manon to learn the trade and occupation of sewing, washing, ironing, and cooking for a term of two years.

Manon Baldwin continued her dealings with her former landlord, Joseph Andrus, selling him land, buying a slave woman from the Lewis Andrus estate with Joseph serving as security for Manon, and appointing him as her agent with power of attorney when she traveled away from Opelousas (St. Landry Parish, Conveyance Book F-1, pp. 428–29). As she grew older and outlived many of her contemporaries, she looked for ways to assure that she would have someone to care for her in her old age. She believed she had found the perfect solution in a couple who rented a small house from her which was located adjacent to her residence. In March 1852, she made a donation and entered into a contractual agreement with Jean-Baptiste and Pauline Defils, free people of color, whereby they agreed to care for her, "ministering to her comforts in health and to her wants in sickness" (St. Landry Parish,

Conveyance Book N-1, pp. 390–91). In exchange for the contract, Manon agreed to grant them, for a term of ten years after the date of her death, the undisturbed use of the house they were living in as well as the lot and house in which she lived (St. Landry Parish, Donation Book 2, pp. 161–62). This arrangement lasted a little more than a year. Apparently something occurred that made it impossible for the Defils couple to fulfill their obligation to Manon. Therefore, on April 2, 1853, they jointly declared the donation and contract null and void (St. Landry Parish, Conveyance Book O-1, pp. 233–34).

Manon had a last will and testament prepared in 1854 (St. Landry Parish, Miscellaneous Book 1, pp. 52–53) and a second one in 1855 (Miscellaneous Book 1, pp. 219–20). In both she insisted that her debts be paid. She made some specific bequests, named Solomon Harmon as her testamentary executor, and bequeathed to him the remainder of her estate after he fulfilled all the terms of her will. She died in December 1857, at the age of eighty-four. The estimative inventory valued her estate at $185.88. When the public auction was held on March 10, 1858, the proceeds of the estate totaled $260.65 (St. Landry Parish, Probate Court Estate 2102). When compared to the more affluent and important free families of color, her life and estate appear insignificant. But when one considers the totality of her life, it becomes apparent that she influenced many lives, and in her own way, she may have been the most liberated member of Opelousas's free black community.

CHAPTER FOUR

Class and Cultural Orientation

The shrewd manipulation of the legal system by nineteenth-century Creoles of Color belies the preeminence of property and the family in their hierarchy of values, characteristics that were also hallmarks of the local Francophone white community. For example, in his last will and testament, drawn up on December 1, 1858, Narcisse Onezime Quatrevaux, a free man of color from St. Landry Parish, granted his wife usufruct of his property but forbade her from alienating, mortgaging, or selling any of that property, which was to be kept intact for his children. Quatrevaux also demanded that his wife "always maintain the buildings and fences in good condition" to protect his heirs' patrimony. Quatrevaux's last will and testament indicates that he was born at Verneuil-sur-Serre, France, on February 23, 1816, to a Frenchman and a slave woman. His mother evidently chose to remain in France following his birth to avoid returning to slave status. Though Quatrevaux's background differed somewhat from those of native-born *gens de couleur libre,* who were also often the product of French men and slave women, his attitudes toward family and property are representative of the group as a whole (St. Landry Parish, Recorder File 3142). Values held in common with local white French-speakers helped to forge the cultural links that quickly came to complement the biological ties binding the black and white Creole communities. By the mid-nineteenth century, the Simiens (sometimes rendered Semiens), Lemelles, Donatos, and other economically successful families had come to share, to a considerable degree, the culture of the white Creole elite, whom they emulated obsessively (MacDonald, Kemp, and Haas 172; Brasseaux 1990:12). This drive toward cultural amalgamation began in the earliest days of the Creole communities' development in the prairie region, when most first-generation free blacks voluntarily abandoned their African names, taking for themselves and their children French given names and giving their children the surnames of their French and white Creole paramours. Creoles of Color also became almost universally Roman Catholic and French-speaking, in emulation of their white counterparts. Most slaves in the region (with the exception of those owned by free persons of color) were Protestant and English-speaking, particularly during the late antebellum period, and these religious and linguistic differences helped to underscore the widening cultural gap between the caste system's second and third tiers. Like white Creoles, the free people of color became preoccupied with their social status, particularly since Louisiana's forced inheritance laws and the resulting difficulty in transmitting wealth from one generation to the next made status difficult to maintain. This problem is evident in the settlement of the estate of Mme. Antoine D. Meuillon (Elizabeth Donato Meuillon) (St. Landry Parish, Conveyance Book U-1, p. 75).

On March 20, 1866, while attempting to settle his late wife's estate, Antoine D. Meuillon reached a preliminary agreement with his children by acknowledging his indebtedness to the estate totaling $13,045.85. This amount consisted of $8,516.05 which his late spouse had inherited from her grandfather Martin Donato, $1,529.80 which she had received from her deceased brother Lucien Donato, and $5,529.80 composing one-half of her community property. In the partial settlement, Antoine gave his children the home place, including ten arpents frontage by fifty-four arpents depth on the right bank of Bayou Teche in Prairie Laurent, six Creole horses and one Creole mule, two pairs of work oxen, thirty head of horned cattle, some farming utensils, and some household furniture. Meuillon estimated the settlement at $9,460 and indicated that he still owed his children $3,585.85. Even with the loss (through freedom) of six slaves, Lucien's estate, valued at $2,724 at the time of his death, had been diminished by only $1,105.

The estate was finally settled on April 17, 1871, by an act of partition through which the heirs divided the property into eight shares. Each received one-eighth of the total bayou frontage, thereby subdividing a once impressive plantation into a collection of small farms. In the donation, Antoine D. Meuillon did not indicate that he retained the usu-fruct of the property until his death, but the fact that the partition did not occur until 1871 indicates that he continued to enjoy the use of his property for some time after his donation (St. Landry Parish, Convey-ance Book Y-1, p. 384).

Antoine Meuillon's actions in transferring title to his property to his children before his death lends insight into the importance of property ownership and the status it provided to members of the Creole of Color community. In a closed society such as the antebellum Creole commu-nity, the economic significance of marriage was thus magnified, as is evident in the marriage contracts (now often called prenuptial agree-ments) drawn up to protect the propertied interests of the prospective marriage partners (Vidrine and De Ville 40–64).

Marital alliances between free blacks were usually carefully arranged to preserve their rank among the local Creoles of color (Hébert vols. 1–6) and had the effect of preserving the group's racial integrity. By the time of the Civil War, the free black population of the Attakapas and Opelousas areas—with the notable exception of St. Landry Parish—was almost universally "mulatto." (By this time legal documents, par-ticularly those written in English, used the word *mulatto* as a generic term for all free people of color.) (Table 7).

TABLE 7

Racial Composition of the Free Black Population of the Attakapas and Opelousas Regions, 1850

Parish	Mulattoes	Percent	Negroes	Percent
Calcasieu	224	99.56	1	.44
Lafayette	156	98.11	3	1.89
St. Landry	1,003	83.44	199	16.56
St. Martin	473	88.74	60	11.26
St. Mary	364	87.92	50	12.08
Vermilion	14	100.00	0	0

Source: 1850 census.

The racial composition and homogeneity of the free black community helped set it apart from the enslaved population, which had remained 70 to 80 percent black. The group's increasingly white cultural orientation made skin color a matter of growing importance to the Creole community (Sterkx 204–7, 213, 246–58).

While embracing many facets of white Creole culture, numerous first-generation free blacks also adopted the economic capitalism of their white neighbors. Fully cognizant that economic failure could result in their return to slave status—as specified by antebellum Louisiana law—the *gens de couleur libre* worked tirelessly to improve their lot.

Like most of their white contemporaries, they believed that economic independence could be obtained only through real estate acquisition and agricultural development. Most at least attempted to acquire land, and many eventually purchased slaves. Slaveholding was especially widespread among the free people of color in the prairie parishes, where the number of black slaveholders and the median size of their slaveholdings mirrored those of the slaveholding segment of the local white population. Indeed, by 1830, the institution of slavery within this black society had reached a level of maturity previously unknown in the rural Deep South. According to the 1830 federal census of Louisiana, 51 Creole of Color slaveholders in the Attakapas and Opelousas areas collectively owned 507 slaves, the largest aggregate black slaveholding in rural Louisiana. This composite figure becomes even more impressive when viewed from a broader perspective. The 1830 federal census indicates that the free black slaveholdings in the Attakapas and Opelousas areas alone eclipsed the statewide totals for free people of color in all but four of the slave states—three if the Louisiana figures were removed. In addition, the average individual slaveholding among Attakapas and Opelousas area free black slaveholders—8.31—was significantly larger than the statewide free black composites for any slaveholding area in the nation (Woodson 1–42).

Such aggressive acquisition of slaves and concomitant personal wealth would, at first glance, seem to lend credence to reports that some free black slaveholders were so obsessed with economic success that they drove their slaves mercilessly. Some contemporary observers maintained that they extracted more work with fewer compensations from their

Negro bondsmen than did their white counterparts (Sterkx 281). In the 1850s, for example, a Virginia-born slave expressed his low opinion of them to traveler Frederick Law Olmsted:

> He said . . . that there were many free negroes all about this region. Some of them were very rich. He pointed out to me three plantations . . . which were owned by colored men. These bought black folks, he said, and had servants of their own. They were very bad masters, very hard and cruel—hadn't any feeling. "You might think master, dat dey would be good to dar own nation; but dey is not. I will tell you de truth, massa . . . dey is very bad masters, sar. I'd rather be a servant to any man in de world, dan to a brack man. If I was sold to a brack man, I'd drown myself" (121).

These statements are corroborated by the findings of historian Loren Schweninger, who has noted that

> like their white neighbors, some [free persons of color] were benevolent masters, granting their blacks special privileges, emancipating especially loyal servants, respecting the sanctity of slave families. But most considered their blacks as chattel property. They bought, sold, mortgaged, willed, traded, and transferred fellow Negroes, demanded long hours in the fields, and severely disciplined recalcitrant blacks. A few seemed as callous as the most profit-minded whites, selling children away from parents, mothers away from husbands, and brutally whipping slaves who ignored plantation rules. On sugar estates, where the harvesting and pressing of the cane demanded, as it did in the Caribbean, sixteen- and eighteen-hour workdays, mulatto owners pushed their slaves incessantly. (348–49)

Such brutality appears to have been confined principally to the river parish area, where free people of color faced greater financial and social pressures for economic success. The documentary record offers no evidence of such a harsh slave regime within southwestern Louisiana's Creole of Color settlements. This is not to say, however, that Attakapas and Opelousas area Creole of Color slaveholders were any less demanding that their white counterparts. To the contrary, the great wealth accumulated by the large free black slaveholders in the prairie region indicates that they drove their workers at least as relentlessly as did neighboring white planters.

Management of slaves was merely one facet of the free blacks' economic and cultural mimicry of white planters. Like members of the white elite, leading free black families valued education, and, like rich whites, they educated their children either by means of tutors or private schools (Dunbar-Nelson 65). H. E. Sterkx notes that in St. Landry Parish, many of the colored planters sent their children to the Grimble Bell school for Free Negroes at Washington, Louisiana. This institution offered instruction on the primary and secondary levels, and it usually enrolled about 125 students. The teaching staff consisted of four instructors, who used the Lancastrian method of teaching. Students attending the school were, as a rule, charged $15 a month for board and tuition. The subjects taught were common to most academies of the nineteenth century and included reading, writing, arithmetic, history, geography, bookkeeping, English, French, and Latin (269–70). Following the destruction of the Grimble Bell school in 1859, "many of the youths of that section of the state [the Opelousas-Washington area] were sent to private schools in New Orleans" (Willey 248).

By the late antebellum period, such cultural emulation had become so successful and so pervasive among economically prosperous free blacks that white Creole planters—particularly those who came into contact with *hommes de couleur libre*—felt an immediate sense of cultural kinship with them. As Sterkx has noted, "Social relationships between well-to-do [free Negro] planters and White planters were usually cordial. When coming into contact with each other for business or other purposes both parties exhibited the amenities characteristic of the 19th century" (282–83). But the impression made by free black planters on their white counterparts went far deeper than the customary exchange of civilities would suggest. An immediate sense of camaraderie developed which tended to dissolve the artificial legal barriers to free association between the white and free black communities. Creole historian Charles Etienne Arthur Gayarré recorded two notable white and Creole encounters in his memoirs. In the first, "riding on a steamboat, a White planter struck up a conversation with a cultured Mulatto grower. When dinnertime arrived, a solitary table was set aside for the latter. Moved by the colored man's quiet acceptance, the White man went to him with a friend: 'We desire you to dine with us.' The free colored man expressed his appreciation for their hospitality, but declined as his presence at their table, even though acceptable to them, might displease the other passengers." In the second encounter, a white traveler who called on a free black acquaintance refused to eat unless his host joined him in the repast, a social encounter not only unacceptable to, but unthinkable for, most antebellum white Louisianians (Gayarré quoted in Sterkx 282–83).

Such limited social equality as the respect and goodwill of white planters afforded was confined largely to those second- and third-generation free blacks who reaped the benefits of their ancestors' investments in land, livestock, and slaves. Perhaps the most notable of these cultured scions of Creole pioneers was Martin Donato Bello, the son of Donato Bello, an Italian-born Opelousas militia officer, and Marie-Jeanne Taillefero, a free mulatto woman (Hébert 1:36). In 1803, Martin Donato Bello and his bride, Marianne Duchesne, established a community of gains and acquets valued in excess of $20,000. Their assets included not only 2,142 arpents of land but also a cotton gin and a small number of slaves. Sometime after 1803 he dropped the Bello from his name and began referring to himself as simply Martin Donato. Over the next fifteen years, Martin Donato expanded the family holdings to 5,096 acres and forty-nine slaves. In 1830, he was the third largest free black slaveholder in the United States, owning seventy-five slaves (Woodson 1–42). At the time of his death in 1848, Martin Donato owned eighty-eight Negro slaves. In addition, the Creole farmer and rancher accumulated so much cash that, in the 1830s and 1840s, he often served as a private banker to local white planters (Baker and Kreamer 78–79).

Creoles of Color of the prairies borrowed not only the agricultural capitalism and life-styles of their role models but their biases as well. By the mid-nineteenth century, successful Creoles—like their white counterparts—had come to consider themselves a social elite. As Sterkx has noted, "Colored aristocrats dressed, thought, and in many ways acted as haughty as their white counterparts towards the 'lowly'" (283–84). Though these attitudes were shared by most members of the antebellum Creole communities in the Attakapas and Opelousas districts, they cannot be said to characterize all of them. As was true of all of the major ethnic and racial groups in early Louisiana, Creoles were not a monolithic group. In fact, the free population schedules of the 1850 census

indicate that local free black society was highly stratified both economically and socially (Table 8). According to the census, four free
black families in south-central and southwest Louisiana owned at least
$10,000 in real estate—an important criterion used by many modern
historians to select members of the planter class. Having the necessary
economic resources and business expertise, successful free blacks participated fully in the prosperity enjoyed by the Attakapas and Opelousas
regions in the 1850s. By 1860, there were seventeen free black planters
in St. Landry Parish alone. Among them were Auguste Donato, who
owned $21,600 worth of real estate as well as sixty slaves valued at
$47,000 (1860 census); the widow Antoine Paillet of St. Landry Parish,
who owned $10,000 in real estate; and Romain Verdun of St. Mary
Parish, who possessed $15,000 in real property (Sterkx 207).

Like many of their white counterparts, members of the free black
elite sought to consolidate their position atop the local socioeconomic
hierarchy through economic diversification. During the late antebellum
period, numerous wealthy free men and women of color entered the
grocery business, either individually or through partnerships. For example, on March 18, 1857, two brothers, Cornelius Donato and Joseph
D. Donato, formalized a partnership to establish a grocery store on the
corner of Court and Bellevue streets in Opelousas (St. Landry Parish,
Partnership Book 2, p. 45).

Most free black landowners, like their white counterparts, possessed
between $50 and $5,000 in real property. Many free blacks who owned
little or no real estate lived in the numerous small towns then developing in the region. In 1850, for example, 80 of the 159 free blacks residing
in Lafayette Parish lived in Vermilionville, the parish seat. These free
persons of color then constituted the largest single element of the town's
free population (Brasseaux 1990:12). Nearly 46 percent of the free black
population in St. Martin Parish lived in the towns of St. Martinville and
New Iberia, while 57 of the 414 free persons of color in St. Mary Parish
resided in Franklin. Unlike their rural counterparts, who usually derived their livelihood from farming or ranching, both as freeholders and
increasingly as day laborers, free black urbanites were usually involved
in the building trades (St. Landry Parish, Civil District Suit 2976),
which would attract increasing numbers of *gens de couleur libre* throughout the prosperous 1850s (Table 9). In addition, most local hotels—and

TABLE 8

Real Estate Holdings by Free Blacks in the Attakapas and Opelousas Districts, 1850

Parish	No real estate	Less than $250	Less than $500	Less than $1,500	Less than $5,000	Less than $10,000	More than $10,000
Calcasieu	35	2	0	1	1	0	0
Lafayette	22	10	1	2	0	0	0
St. Landry	247	23	14	18	9	0	2
St. Martin	79	3	7	11	7	1	0
Vermilion	0	0	1	0	0	0	1

Source: 1850 census.

T A B L E 9

Occupations of Free Blacks in the Attakapas
and Opelousas Regions, 1850

Occupation	Number	Percent
Baker	1	0.35
Blacksmith	4	1.39
Bricklayer	3	1.05
Butcher	3	1.05
Carpenter	34	11.85
Cartwright	1	0.35
Clerk	3	1.05
Convict	1	0.35
Farmer	123	42.86
Grazer (Rancher)	22	7.67
Laborer	85	29.62
Mechanic	1	0.35
Saddler	1	0.35
Shoemaker	2	0.70
Storekeeper	1	0.35
Tavern keeper	1	0.35
Teacher	1	0.35

Source: 1850 census.

many local houses of prostitution (Barde 335)—would come to be owned and operated by free blacks in the last decade of the antebellum period. Free persons of color also owned and operated numerous local coffeehouses (St. Landry Parish, Miscellaneous Book 2, p. 85). Like their rural counterparts, the urban Creoles sought to improve their status economically, and many of them would eventually become small slaveholders (1850 census, slave schedules).

Contrary to oral tradition among the Creoles of Color in the prairie and Teche Valley parishes, most slave acquisitions by free persons of color were not thinly veiled attempts to liberate or, at the very least, improve the living conditions of enslaved spouses, children, and other relatives. In the early years of the nineteenth century, some members of embryonic Creole of Color community, particularly recently manumitted men, appear to have purchased wives, children, and mothers to liberate them from captivity (Interview of Mary Ellen Donato by Claude Oubre, 1971). Of the forty slaves purchased in St. Martin Parish by free persons of color between 1800 and 1820, thirteen (32 percent) were women, eighteen (45 percent), were children, and only six (15 percent) were men. The remaining three slaves were not identified. During this same period, *gens de couleur libre* manumitted twenty-one individuals: three men (14 percent), four women (19 percent), and fourteen children (67 percent). It is equally noteworthy, however, that nineteen of the forty slaves purchased by free persons of color remained in bondage and that eight (20 percent) of these individuals were subsequently sold again (St. Martin Parish Original Acts, vols. 22–28).

The number of slaves in the latter category, who were obviously acquired as permanent slaves, became proportionately larger as the antebellum period progressed, particularly among the oldest free black families, who had grown accustomed to slave ownership. Many black slaveholders, like their white counterparts, appear to have regarded bondsmen as mere chattel to be bought and sold like any other commodity. Their expedient Reconstruction protestations of solidarity with freedmen notwithstanding, many Creole of Color slave owners in the prairie parishes continued to buy, sell, and trade human beings throughout the Civil War. Slaves in these transactions were often sold to whites, sometimes at exorbitant prices. Indeed, the average price of a slave sold in these wartime conveyances was $1,615 (St. Landry Parish, Conveyance Book T-1, pp. 72, 169, 252, 610). The attitude of these black slaveholders is perhaps best exemplified by the postwar legal wrangling between the heirs of Carlostin Auzenne and Hypolite Mallet. Both men had been slave-owning free persons of color before the attack on Fort Sumter, and, on December 17, 1859, Mallet had purchased slaves from Auzenne. By late 1866, Mallet still owed Auzenne $2,248 from the slave conveyance, and, despite the abolition of slavery, the heirs of Auzenne, who died on November 3, 1865, filed suit to collect the debt. The Auzenne family ultimately accepted a settlement of $2,000 (Hardy 192).

There are, however, documented cases of humanitarian slave purchases in the late antebellum period. In 1855, for example, Zenon Rideau purchased for $700 a mulatto slave girl named Aimi (probably Aimée) to be the bride of Rideau's eldest son, Jean-Baptiste Rideau. Because children inherited their mother's status (i.e., free or slave) under contemporary Louisiana law, Zenon Rideau subsequently asked the St. Landry Parish District Court to emancipate Aimi so that his grandchildren would be born free. A writ of emancipation was issued by the court in 1856, three weeks after Ozelia, Zenon's first grandchild, was born; obviously apprised of the birth, the parish judge adjudicated Ozelia free also (St. Landry Parish, Civil District Suit 7646).

Other slaves were freed by *hommes de couleur libre* under circumstances strikingly reminiscent of the emancipation of their ancestors. For example, Martin Donato's last will and testament, written on September 2, 1847, provides for the manumission of Julie, a thirty-two-year-old mulatress, and her seven children, Eugenie, fourteen years of age; Emile, twelve; Uranie, eleven; Feliciane and Felicie, twin sisters, eight; Philomene, four; and Didier, one year and three months old. Martin Donato's wife had died in 1832, and it appears that Julie had become his concubine and had provided him with seven children. Most of these children are subsequently identified as Donatos in local conveyance records, which corroborates this supposition (St. Landry Parish, Alienation Record Book 1, pp. 75–76).

Martin Donato not only ordered Julie and her children freed, but he also made provisions for their subsequent care, naming his son Auguste as curator of the minor children and ordering him to handle Julie's financial affairs and those of her children. Such supervision, Martin Donato evidently felt, was necessary because of the substantial sums of money he bequeathed to Julie and her children. Upon Martin's death, Julie received $2,000 to be used for the acquisition of furniture. (Auguste was ordered to consider the furnishings in Julie's room as her legal property.) Julie's children received an additional $2,100, which, Martin Donato hoped, would assure them a profession or dowry (St. Landry Parish, Alienation Record Book 1, pp. 75–76).

Martin Donato, one of the largest slaveholders in St. Landry Parish, also provided for the emancipation of several slaves, one of whom appears to have been the child of his son Edmond. To ensure that his wishes were honored, Donato added two stipulations to his will. The first prohibited his legal heirs and the executor of his estate from selling any of the foregoing slaves before they could be emancipated by listing them in his succession inventory. The second mandated that any of his children or grandchildren who dared to contest the will would be disinherited. It is hardly necessary to add that Martin Donato's wishes were carried out to the letter (St. Landry Parish, Alienation Book 1, pp. 75–76).

The disputed Dennis Lemelle succession describes a similar attempt to manumit slave relatives, but with dramatically different results. In this episode, there were two conflicting wills, one of which provided for the emancipation of several slaves. Lemelle's legitimate heirs successfully challenged the second will and blocked the liberation of the slaves he had evidently sought to release (St. Landry Parish, Probate Suite 45).

Despite the financial assistance provided by many of their fathers, newly emancipated free men and women of color generally occupied a lower socioeconomic niche than their more established confrères. But despite the disparities of social status and wealth among individuals within the free black community, the perception among whites was that the *gens de couleur libre* were generally wealthy and thus a threat to white superiority. This view was not entirely without basis. Like local whites, free persons of color in the prairie region enjoyed unprecedented prosperity during the 1850s, and, according to Schweninger, the number of "relatively prosperous [free black] real-estate owners" possessing "at least $2,000 in realty" between 1850 and 1860 tripled in St. Landry Parish, nearly quadrupled in St. Martin Parish, and nearly doubled in St. Mary Parish: St. Landry Parish, eight to twenty-five; St. Martin Parish, four to fifteen; St. Mary Parish, eight to thirteen (Schweninger 350). Cumulative property holdings of free blacks in Lafayette Parish nearly doubled during the decade, rising from $5,700 to $10,500. Average property holdings of free persons of color in these parishes in 1860 were as follows: St. Landry, $1,852; St. Martin, $2,542; St. Mary, $5,170; and Lafayette, $618 (Schweninger 362–63). As tensions in the region increased as a result of the slavery controversy in the 1850s, free blacks increasingly became a target for whites frustrated with the South's limited ability to defend the "peculiar institution" through normal political channels. St. Landry's free black community, the largest in the prairie region, bore the brunt of the assault.

CHAPTER FIVE

Vigilantes, Jayhawkers, and Postbellum Hard Times

Crystallizing in the late 1850s, white hostility to local free blacks took the form of legal and extralegal efforts to eradicate the free black population—by intimidation if possible, violence if necessary. Responding to the escalating threat, many free blacks fled the prairies for Latin America. As early as 1832, members of St. Landry Parish's Donato family began to forge cultural and economic ties with the Veracruz region of Mexico (Baker and Kreamer 83). Lucien Donato, who established the Creoles' Mexican connection, invested his share of his grandmother's estate in a modest agricultural operation that eventually prospered sufficiently to permit the St. Landry native to amass an estate valued at $2,724 by his death in 1851. Among Donato's possessions were six slaves, twenty-five horses, an ox cart, a double-barreled shotgun, carpenter's tools, bed and bedding, a tub, a table, four mules, and two Creole ponies (St. Landry Parish, Estate 1545). The long-term importance of these contacts, however, would not be fully realized by the free blacks of the prairies until the late 1850s (Sterkx 292–95).

The initial attempt to eradicate the free Negroes from south Louisiana had consisted of the peaceful efforts of the Louisiana Colonization Society to "repatriate" free persons of color to their African "fatherland." At the height of the society's repatriation activities in the late antebellum period, however, few free blacks—now firmly established second- and third-generation Louisianians for the most part—expressed any interest in leaving their native state, despite the rising racial tensions in the prairie parishes during the 1840s and 1850s. Only 309 "free colored emigrants" from Louisiana were transplanted in Liberia between 1831 and 1860 (Sterkx 295–96).

The resistance to Liberian colonization among the state's free black population caused Louisiana's advocates of black colonization to laud Mexico's virtues as a potential site. Partisans of sending Louisiana free blacks to Mexico solicited financial assistance from the federal government, but no funds materialized. Nevertheless, many Louisiana free blacks—most of them former Attakapas and Opelousas residents— made their way to the Veracruz area. The vanguard of this colony consisted of an undetermined number of St. Landry Parish expatriates, led by members of the Donato family, who reportedly carried with them "a considerable fortune and technical equipment which promised to make the experiment a success." Settling along the Popolopan River, these colonists proved so successful at growing Indian corn that they soon began to invite relatives to join them in a country where, they claimed, there was less racial animosity than in their native state. Few Louisiana relatives, however, heeded this call to migrate until 1859, when numerous armed bands of vigilantes began their reign of terror in southwest Louisiana (Barde 337).

Acadiana's *comités de vigilance* were created in response to the local judicial system's failure to apprehend or convict numerous petty criminals responsible for a crime wave that swept the prairie country in the late 1850s. Local white property owners organized themselves into paramilitary groups of night riders who tried alleged criminals in absentia and, after apprehending their unsuspecting victims at their homes during nocturnal raids, executed sentence—usually a flogging followed by a warning to leave the country under penalty of death. Striking often and without warning, the vigilantes quickly drove much of the local criminal element into exile in Texas or the western Louisiana prairies. The vigilantes then turned their attention to local residents deemed undesirable either because of their unpopular political views or their flagrant disregard for social conventions. European immigrants suspected of socialistic political tendencies, poor whites who had slave or free black concubines, free blacks with slave lovers, and poor persons of all walks of life and all racial backgrounds who openly defied the social controls maintained by the planter caste were victimized by the vigilantes (Sterkx 285–315).

Free blacks were not spared the vigilante onslaught, and, as in white society, the lower economic orders of that community appear to have been the primary targets for vigilante terrorism. One of the raids most celebrated by the vigilantes was against the Coco settlement at Anse-la-Butte, in St. Martin Parish. Coco, a free Negro, had, for nearly fifty years, openly maintained a polygamous, extramarital relationship with two white sisters, by whom he had nineteen children. Coco and his sole remaining wife appear to have briefly enjoyed a peaceful existence until the organization of the vigilante Committee of Pont de la Butte. The children settled alongside the parents, establishing a village called Cocoville. The sons lived off the land as hunters and trappers, but the daughters, according to vigilante sources, supported themselves by prostitution. It was through prostitution that members of the Coco family reportedly became associated with various white "undesirables" who were among the first victims of the second phase of vigilante repression.

The actual cause of the vigilante crusade against this multiracial community was, and remains, the subject of considerable debate. Coco maintained that the vigilantes coveted his land. The night riders insisted that land was not an issue, asserting that the polygamous feature of Coco's extramarital, interracial relationship was the source of their ire. They also claimed to object both to the lax morals of Coco's mulatto daughters and to the petty thefts allegedly committed by their white male customers to pay for the daughters' sexual favors (Barde chap. 5).

Sometime in late February or early March 1859, a large party of vigilantes rode to the Cocoville settlement in Prairie Maronne and presented the community's "black Mormon" patriarch with a "decree of exile." Acknowledging the futility of resistance, the Coco family migrated to the Marksville area over the course of the next month, with many junior members of the family finding new homes along the way. Coco, accompanied by five or six clan members, occupied a leaky, abandoned hut, only to be displaced once again by local white vigilantes. Subsequently chased still again from Rapides Parish, Coco and his much maligned family eventually found a haven in New Orleans (Barde chap. 5).

Many other free blacks of the Attakapas and Opelousas districts were also forced to abandon their homes, but, unlike Coco's family, they often tasted the lash before enduring exile. Every attempt at resistance was crushed, and despite the vigilantes' public disavowal of violent intentions against "respectable" free people of color, many innocent free blacks were sufficiently intimidated to join the exodus. Like Coco's family, most of the refugees seem to have made their way to the Crescent City. Among the first emigrants to reach the city were one hundred exiles from St. Landry Parish, where inflammatory editorials by the *Opelousas Patriot*—"the most violent anti-Negro organ in [antebellum] Louisiana"—had spurred local vigilantes into a frenzy of anti-free-black activity focused primarily against the Creoles of Color. By 1860 St. Landry night riders had forced the Grimble Bell school at Washington to close, prompting many displaced black Creole students to seek an education in New Orleans's private schools for free people of color (Willey 248; Sterkx 302, 304–5, 310; Barde chap. 5).

Terrorism was augmented by legal intimidation. In 1859, a group of prominent white St. Landry Parish planters unsuccessfully lobbied the state legislature to ban slave ownership by free persons of color, which they described as "repugnant to the laws of good society, good government, Nature and Nature's God" (Schweninger 349–50).

Capitalizing on the situation, the Haitian consul at New Orleans, P. E. Desdunes, a free man of color, began to recruit free black refugees from Attakapas and Opelousas for resettlement in Haiti. Desdunes offered as inducements for Haitian settlement free transportation to the black republic and assurances of social equality and political rights and opportunities unavailable to them in Louisiana. Swayed by Desdunes's promises, 150 free blacks—most of them apparently from St. Landry Parish—boarded ships for Haiti in May 1859. An additional 195 free people of color from St. Landry and East Baton Rouge parishes sailed for the island the following month. Emigration to Haiti continued, though on a smaller scale, into early 1860, when at least 80 Opelousas free blacks emigrated to the island republic (Schweninger 302–3; Barde; *Opelousas Courier*, June 14, 1859; *New Orleans Daily Picayune*, January 15, 1860; *Opelousas Journal*, August 6, 1870).

Few participants in this exodus found Haiti to their liking, and many—though not all—returned to New Orleans by the end of the summer of 1859. Yet some of those who remained in Haiti appear to have prospered. Ch. Boisdor (evidently Charles Boisdoré of St. Martin Parish), for example, reportedly became chief armorer for the Haitian government's Port-au-Prince arsenal by 1861 (Sterkx 302–5; Barde).

Though disillusioned by the Haitian experiment, the emigrants were unable to return to their home parishes because of the continued vigilante activity. At least eighty *gens de couleur libre* remained in Haiti until July 1870, when they sailed to New Orleans as a group aboard the *Jeannette* (Sterkx 30–5). On August 6, 1870, the editor of the *Opelousas Journal* reported that these haggard travelers, who arrived "in impoverished circumstances," had already begun to reestablish themselves in their home parish. Many other Opelousas and Attakapas expatriates, however, chose to join the free black colony near Veracruz. Some of the colonists there became merchants, engaging in trade with New Orleans (Barde 337–38; Sterkx 297–98).

As storm clouds gathered over the increasingly volatile slavery issue—and by extension the issue of race relations—free blacks in southwestern Louisiana increasingly found themselves targets of white violence. In the twilight of the antebellum period, most of this violence was confined geographically to the upper Teche region and socially to the lower strata of the free black community. Free black planters on the lower Teche, apparently in an effort to remain in the good graces of the local white population, reportedly contributed to the formation of Confederate military units. No such effort at good faith seems to have been made by the free black planters of St. Martin, Lafayette, and St. Landry parishes, and free blacks generally appear to have maintained a low profile throughout the prairie country when war came in 1861.

The exodus of Confederate volunteers in 1861 and the conscription of many Attakapas and Opelousas poor whites into the rebel army the following year greatly diminished the threat of violence to southwest Louisiana's free black population. New threats, however, appeared in the form of two devastating Union invasions of the Teche Valley in 1863, the simultaneous formation of Jayhawker bands—paramilitary groups of conscription evaders who lived off the land—and, in 1864, an attempt by the state's Confederate government to conscript Attakapas and Opelousas free blacks for duty as forced laborers in north Louisiana. Though some prominent Creoles of Color, such as Auguste Donato, *fils,* evidently entered the Confederate service at this juncture and actively assisted the rebel war effort, most free black males chose to resist impressment (St. Landry Parish, Civil District Suit 9454). Following the onset of conscription of free blacks, free men of color in St. Landry Parish were admitted into the largest and most active Jayhawker group in southwestern Louisiana—the Bois Mallet band commanded by

Ozémé Carrière. Before the Civil War, Carrière had entered into an extramarital liaison with a sister of Martin Guillory, a prominent local free man of color, who, in 1864, became Carrière's chief lieutenant. Following Carrière's assassination by Confederate forces in 1865, Guillory accepted a Union commission as captain and organized his Jayhawkers into the Mallet Free Scouts.

Under the leadership of Carrière and Guillory, the southwest Louisiana Jayhawkers were a formidable fighting force capable of resisting repeated Confederate efforts to annihilate them. Operating out of camps in the Bois Mallet area near present-day Eunice, Louisiana, the Jayhawkers controlled most of the southwestern Louisiana prairie country for much of 1863, 1864, and 1865. While publicly espousing the Confederate cause, St. Landry's wealthiest Creoles of Color appear to have privately supported the insurgents. It is hardly coincidental that such leading free men of color as Auguste Donato, *fils,* capitalized on the Jayhawker presence to move as many of their increasingly valuable cotton bales as possible to relatives' farms in the Bois Mallet area, where they would be safe from Confederate and Union foragers. Indeed, contemporary civil suits indicate that free men of color were even transporting to Jayhawker territory fencing materials that they acquired from Union forces.

Solomon B. Harmon, a white man, sued Firman Lemelle, a former free man of color, in 1866 over one such incident. According to Harmon's complaint, in April 1863, Federal troops under the command of General Nathaniel P. Banks removed all the fencing materials from his plantation and transported them to their campsite near Firman Lemelle's property. Upon the invaders' departure, Lemelle allegedly moved the surviving materials—estimated to include 1,500 *pieux,* horizontal fence posts nine feet long with tennons cut, and 300 vertical fence posts, also nine feet long but with precut mortises—to his farmstead. Harmon asked the court to force Lemelle either to surrender the fencing materials or to pay him $350, their estimated value. Unfortunately, the court's disposition was not appended to the complaint (St. Landry Parish, Civil District Suit 10150).

It is equally significant that, though the Jayhawkers lived off the land by pillaging local farms, particularly those between Opelousas and Church Point, they appear to have scrupulously avoided the caches of agricultural stores hidden by free persons of color at Bois Mallet. Indeed, at a time when Jayhawkers were conducting daring daylight raids against Cajun yeomen, Auguste Donato's cotton bales sat abandoned but untouched on Evariste Guillory's Bois Mallet farm.

Jayhawker partisanship would eventually cost the anti-Confederates dearly. The destructive, usually violent Jayhawker raids in the last two years of the Civil War not only eroded the insurgents' local base of support but also generated a tremendous grass-roots backlash within southwestern Louisiana's free population. Shortly after the cessation of hostilities, a group of white and black men assassinated Martin Guillory at his home near Opelousas.

Guillory's assassination signaled the beginning of a new and violent chapter in the history of southwestern Louisiana—one that would see an escalation of vigilante activities in the rural areas for the duration of the postbellum era and throughout the 1880s. But at the end of the Civil War, most free blacks in the Attakapas and Opelousas areas were less concerned with the threat of violence than with their changing economic and social status. Like their white neighbors, free black property holders endured the devastating effects of long-term foraging by the Confederate and Union armies; the widespread destruction and theft of private property by unruly soldiers and camp followers; the expropriation of property, produce, and livestock by the Confederate and Federal governments; the depreciation of Confederate currency; and the emancipation of slaves (Brasseaux 1992:chaps. 5–7). Many free black men and women of substance before the war found themselves impoverished at the war's conclusion (Table 10).

Numerous free men and women of color somehow managed to preserve a significant portion of their wealth during the war, evidently by hiding valuable agricultural produce behind Jayhawker lines and then selling these commodities in the enormously lucrative early postwar market. Even those individuals whose estates suffered heavy wartime depreciation retained important buying power, and they used this economic clout to advantage during the war and in the early Reconstruction period.

Some of the most enterprising members of the former free black community viewed the collapse of local real estate values as an unprecedented opportunity to speculate in undervalued farmlands. A startlingly

TABLE 10

A Comparison of the Antebellum and Postbellum Property Holdings
of the Most Prominent Free Blacks, St. Landry Parish, 1860–1870

Name	Property 1860	Property 1870
Donato, Auguste, *père*	68,000	6,000
Meuillon, Antoine D.[a]	56,100	9,460
Meullion, Alphonse[b]	44,460	N/A
Meullion, Belasire	28,000	N/A
Guillory, Evariste	26,520	2,500
Guillory, Donate	23,790	1,800
Guillory, Casimire	21,296	1,700
Simon, Edouard[c]	19,130	N/A
Rideau, Zenon	16,600	3,000
Simien, François	15,550	2,150
St. Andre, Antoine	13,000	1,100
Galot, Jean	12,800	N/A
Lachapelle, Joseph	11,500	1,800
Beller, Olivrel	10,800	N/A
Fusillier, Edouard	10,800	N/A
Lemel, Alexandre	10,600	N/A
Ozenne, Felix	10,400	1,250
Roujeau, Casimire	10,200	N/A
Wykoff, Edouard	9,000	N/A
Luculus, Elie	8,800	N/A

continued

large number of real estate acquisitions were made by the former *gens de couleur libre* in the wake of the Civil War. In the sampling of annotated land transactions printed in Appendix B, members of nine of the more prominent Creole of Color families in St. Landry Parish are identified as vendees (purchasers) in 128 (80.5 percent) of the 159 conveyance records directly involving them between 1865 and 1881. (In 76 of the 159 transactions [46.49 percent], Creole of Color vendees purchased land from other members of their caste.)

The most notable of these postbellum land sales occurred in 1875,

TABLE 10

Continued

Name	Property 1860	Property 1870
Fontenot, Alphonse	8,500	N/A
Guillory, Caliste	8,400	N/A
Robin, Magdeleine	7,500	N/A
Lemelle, Rigebert	7,500	N/A
Cesaire, Cyprien	6,200	N/A
Gordon, Felisan	5,700	N/A
Donato, J.	5,500	900
Fontenot, Mary Beller	3,450	0
Gantt, George	2,900	N/A
Escadron, Aspasie	2,175	N/A

Source: 1860 and 1870 censuses.

[a] In 1869 Antoine D. Meuillon transferred most of his property to his children. At the time of the donation, this property was valued at $9,460, considerably less than the $56,100 which Meuillon owned in 1860. Antoine D. Meuillon does not appear in the 1870 census.

[b] N/A indicates not listed in the 1870 census of St. Landry Parish. Some of the missing individuals are known to have moved away from St. Landry Parish during the violent upheaval of 1859.

[c] Edouard Simon does not appear in the 1870 census of St. Landry Parish, but Pierre Simon, perhaps an heir of Edouard, is listed with real property holdings valued at $4,000 and personal property worth $500.

when the estate of Auguste Donato, *père,* was sold at public auction for $11,426.89. The property was subdivided and sold in forty-two separate lots averaging about forty-two acres for farmland and about ten acres for woodland. Prices varied from a low of $2.75 per acre to a high of $19.50 per acre (St. Landry Parish, Conveyance Book C-2, pp. 588–95). The seven purchasers included whites and Creoles of Color. It is interesting that none of Donato's children purchased any of the property but chose instead to sell it. This was highly unusual for that time, but when one considers the political activities of the Donatos and their need to secure the votes of the masses of the freedmen, it is plausible to assume that the partition of the agricultural land into roughly forty-acre tracts may have been an attempt to identify with the needs and desires of the freedmen. Unfortunately, at the auction, freedmen were outbid by their white and Creole of Color neighbors (Oubre 1978:52–55).

In these postbellum land transactions, the vendees spent an average of $789.76, a large amount of money in the turbulent early postwar years, when currency was in short supply and the regional credit system was a shambles. The median purchase price is even more impressive when one considers that prime farm lands near the navigable streams and towns could be purchased "at from $10 to $15 per acre; at a distance from the centre of business, at $6 and $3 per acre; in the western portion of the parish, at $2.50 and $1.25" (*Franklin Planters' Banner*, March 23, 1870). These purchases become more impressive still when one considers that because of the economic instability ravaging the prairie parish area, many vendors demanded payment in gold or greenbacks, *extremely* scarce commodities (St. Landry Parish, Conveyance Book U-1, p. 464). Between 1865 and 1876, Creole of Color vendees in St. Landry Parish acquired a total of 4,494.61 arpents, approximately four times the amount sold (1,409.71 arpents) by members of the former free black community during the same period.

This aggressive pattern of land acquisition continued beyond the end of Reconstruction. The properties—constituting 3,099.68 arpents—acquired by Creoles of Color between 1877, the last year of Reconstruction, and 1882 constitute 41 percent of the fifteen-year postbellum total. Indeed, the totals for 1878 and 1879 easily dwarfed those for the busiest Reconstruction years, indicating that economically the Creole of Color elite was relatively unaffected by the state's dramatically changing political environment (Table 11).

Yet this flurry of postwar land acquisitions belied underlying local economic problems that would eventually bring the Creole of Color community to its knees. Though land acquisitions by Creoles of Color remained surprisingly strong throughout the postwar depression, peaking in periods of greatest economic distress, progressively fewer black Creole speculators found themselves profiting from their acquisitions because they fell prey to the pernicious consequences of financial overextension. By 1876, many formerly prominent St. Landry Creoles of

TABLE II

Real Estate Conveyances Involving Creoles of Color, St. Landry
Parish, 1866–1881[a]

Year	Bought land	Total arpents	Sold land	Total arpents
1866	12	442.24	2	457.75
1867	13	936.68	0	0.00
1868	7	226.25	0	0.00
1869	6	454.50	1	30.00
1870	4	94.00	2	176.36
1871	5	96.24	1	390.50
1872	17	816.70	1	20.00
1873	10	419.00	1	0.50
1874	5	127.50	1	0.50
1875	3	458.00	4	136.50
1876	10	423.50	4	197.50
1877	7	129.50	4	125.50
1878	10	1,103.00	4	47.00
1879	11	1,434.68	3	50.50
1880	6	122.50	1	50.00
1881	2	310.00	2	94.00
TOTALS	128	7,594.29	31	1,776.71

Source: St. Landry Parish, Conveyance Books, 1866–81.
[a] In this table, town lots for which no size was given were estimated at 0.5 arpents, the
approximate size of those town lot transactions in which dimensions were specified.

Color were penniless, besieged by creditors, and faced with the prospect
of bankruptcy.

The changing fortunes of the Creoles of Color during Reconstruction are evident in the financial and legal transactions of Edgard Vanhille. During the Civil War, Vanhille purchased land in Opelousas on
at least two occasions. On July 18, 1863, he paid $90 for a lot in the
Louallier addition, then on March 14, 1864, he purchased two arpents
of land in Opelousas for $2,000 cash (St. Landry Parish, Conveyance

Book U-1, pp. 571, 624). On December 2, 1865, in partnership with John Simms, Edgard Vanhille paid Lucius Dupré (the husband of Vanhille's white half-sister) $1,200 for a lot, with all improvements, adjacent to the courthouse square on the corner of Market and Bellevue (St. Landry Parish, Conveyance Book U-1, p. 700). On this location they opened a retail liquor establishment (saloon), which they operated together until September 1866, when Vanhille sold his share of the partnership to Simms for $880.26 (St. Landry Parish, Conveyance Book U-1, p. 212).

In the interim, Edgard Vanhille had bid $600 for one lot and $300 for a second lot from the Larcade estate on Lombard Street, where he established a grocery business (St. Landry Parish, Probate 2804). To help cover some of his costs, he sold a fractional lot, adjacent to the store, to Edward Jackson (former FMC) for $150 on August 18, 1866 (St. Landry Parish, Conveyance Book U-1, p. 198). Then, on November 16, 1867, he sold to Guillaume Fontenot (former FMC) lots in Opelousas measuring two by three arpents, or a total of six superficial arpents, for $235 (St. Landry Parish, Conveyance Book U-1, p. 634).

When Vanhille purchased the two lots from the Larcade estate, he had signed three notes of $300 each, payable at one-year intervals. He apparently failed to meet his payments when the notes matured because on August 15, 1868, he exchanged the mortgage he held for $883.26 on the property he had sold to John Simms, with Block and Dupré, who held the $900 notes he had made to Mrs. Noel Larcade (St. Landry Parish, Miscellaneous Book 4, p. 187).

Edgard Vanhille's land speculation was not restricted to urban property. On September 22, 1866, almost immediately after selling out to Simms, he purchased two tracts of land from Celeste Lastrapes, Rice Garland's widow, for $3,500 (St. Landry Parish, Conveyance Book U-1, p. 240). The first tract, containing two hundred arpents, was located two miles west of Opelousas. The second, containing fifty arpents, was located approximately four miles west of the first tract. He apparently paid nothing down and signed three notes for $1,166.66, each payable at one-year intervals for three years (St. Landry Parish, Mortgage Book 10, p. 414). On August 29, 1868, Armand Wartelle, who was then in possession of the notes, filed suit in District Court indicating that the first of the three notes had matured and that in spite of numerous demands, Vanhille had refused to make payment (St. Landry Parish, Civil District Suit 10974). He also pointed out that the second note would mature on September 22, 1867, and he did not anticipate any more success in collecting from Vanhille. He therefore requested that the land be seized and sold to pay the outstanding notes. Although court records indicate that Wartelle won an order to have the property seized and sold, no evidence exists that the sheriff ever fulfilled the court order. Vanhille apparently held the land until April 4, 1870, when he and Mrs. Garland executed an act of retrocession (St. Landry Parish, Conveyance Book X-1, p. 421). He indicated in this act that he was unable to make the payments he had agreed to and requested that the original act of purchase be declared null and void. He apparently enjoyed the usufruct of the land rent-free for four years; any improvements made during this time remained with the land.

On August 30, 1871, Edgard Vanhille repurchased from Guillaume Fontenot, for $131, the six superficial arpent group of lots he had sold to him in 1867. Since Fontenot had paid Vanhille $235, Vanhille made a profit of $105 on this second transaction. This appears to be the last transaction in which Vanhille was the purchaser.

Unfortunately for Vanhille, his failure to pay bills began to take its toll. On October 17, 1871, the state of Louisiana seized, for nonpayment of taxes, the two lots on Lombardy Street where he operated a grocery and hardware enterprise (St. Landry Parish, Mortgage Book 13, p. 386). At the public auction held on November 14, 1871, Estelle Giron, Vanhille's wife, entered the high bid of $97.55 to redeem her husband's property (St. Landry Parish, Conveyance Book Z-1, p. 6).

Two years later, on August 25, 1873, Vanhille sold the billiard table from his saloon to Adolphe Donato for $200 cash (St. Landry Parish, Miscellaneous Book 5, p. 363). Then, on January 12, 1874, he sold, for the sum of $1,500, to Eloise Chenier, wife of Henri Giron, the two lots he had purchased from the Larcade estate (St. Landry Parish, Conveyance Book B-2, p. 142). According to the terms of the sale, he was paid $1,236.84 cash. Chenier held the last of the $300 notes Vanhille had made on the original purchase. He still owed $253.16 on that note. This sale was apparently precipitated by a suit filed on January 3, 1874, by Alexandre Landry of the firm of Landry and Godefroy for partial non-payment of $2,386.50 for goods and merchandise. In addition to the goods and merchandise, they had also paid out for Vanhille the sum of $203.50. The court documents stipulate that Vanhille had made various payments totaling $1,770.50. The suit requested payment with interest on the unpaid balance, which Landry calculated at $907.41. On February 9, 1874, Landry was granted a judgment for the above amount (St. Landry Parish, Civil District Court Suit 12372). In anticipation of the judgment, Vanhille sold to Alexandre LeJeune the contents of the storehouse on the corner of North and Lombardy, containing a "lot of hardware, glassware, shelving, counters" for $100 (St. Landry Parish, Miscellaneous Book 5, p 436). This action apparently ended Vanhille's mercantile ventures.

Although he had lost some of his income-producing urban property, Vanhille and his wife still possessed both urban and rural property. In 1875 and 1876, Mrs. Vanhille leased a portion of her plantation, including a sugar house, to Dominique Lalanne. The 1876 lease stipulated that the $200 lease payment was to be made to John Chaffe Bros., who were Mrs. Vanhille's creditors (St. Landry Parish, Miscellaneous Book 6, p. 297). That same year, Vanhille, acting as agent for his wife, leased another portion of the plantation, known as the old Donato tract, to Jean Lastrapes. Lastrapes "binds himself to pay to said Vanhille two bales of cotton of this years crop of not less than 400 pounds weight each—or its equivalent in corn fodder, potatoes, etc. The said Vanhille is also to furnish free to the said Lastrapes one pair of oxen to make the crop" (St. Landry Parish, Mortgage Book 17, p. 125).

A crop lien signed by Edgard Vanhille with David Roos on April 12, 1877, indicates the financial straits in which Vanhille found himself. The document states: "On the 1st of Nov. 1877, I promise to pay to the order of David Roos, fifty dollars amount now due and to be advanced to me during the year 1877 in necessary supplies to cultivate land of my own for which advances I grant said David Roos full privileges on all crops raised by me or by any member of my family or by any one employed by me in making a crop on said land this year 1877, said Roos reserves the right of issuing these supplies on a monthly [basis], and at his option to decrease the amount above specified according to prospects of crops" (St. Landry Parish, Mortgage Book 17, p. 591). Once a land speculator and prosperous merchant, Vanhille was reduced to dependency on others to plant a crop on his own land.

Economic casualties such as Edgard Vanhille were, like hundreds of their white neighbors, simply unable to endure the effects of repeated natural and economic disasters that plagued south-central Louisiana between 1866 and 1877 (Schweninger 353–64). And like their white counterparts, these former free black landholders gradually lost their economic independence (Brasseaux 1992:chaps. 5–7).

The increasing number of child indentures among the former *gens de couleur libre* during the Reconstruction era bear poignant testimony to the worsening economic crisis. The example of Marcella Lemelle is most illuminating. By the end of Reconstruction, Marcella's evidently widowed mother, a member of a former leading free black family in St. Landry Parish, was apparently no longer capable of supporting and educating her. Lemelle was consequently reduced to entering an indenture agreement with Opelousas merchant Joseph Bloch on January 11, 1878. Under the terms of this agreement, approved by Marcella's mother, the child "bound and put herself servant to said Joseph Bloch, [and] his wife . . . to serve them . . . during the term of ten years, . . . during all of which time said Marcella Lemelle binds herself faithfully to serve, and that honestly and obediently in all things as a good & dutiful servant ought to do." In return for this "good & dutiful" service, Lemelle would receive "sufficient meat and drink, lodging, apparel, and suitable medical attention in case of sickness," as well as "the opportunity of instruction in the rudiments of an English education" (St. Landry Parish, Miscellaneous Book 6, p. 515).

Compounding the devastating economic impact of the war was the sudden dissolution of the legal and social systems underpinning the privileged social position of the free blacks in Louisiana's three-tier caste system. The emancipation of Negro slaves eradicated the legal distinctions that had helped to set the *gens de couleur libre* apart. Local black codes, such as the one adopted, but only briefly enforced, in Opelousas in July 1865, treated blacks as though they were a monolithic group and endowed them all with the highly circumscribed rights of freedmen (the recently emancipated slaves). That Creoles of Color now constituted a tiny minority of the region's African-American population compounded the identity crisis spawned by their postbellum loss of legal status.

Most of the former members of the free black community rebelled against its loss of status and the resulting inevitability of social amalgam-

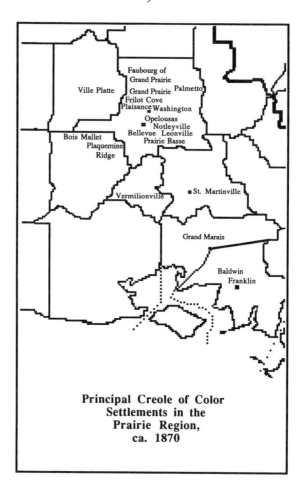

**Principal Creole of Color
Settlements in the
Prairie Region,
ca. 1870**

ation with the freedmen, from whom they had tried so long to distance themselves. To distinguish themselves from their social inferiors, the former free blacks began to identify themselves locally as Creoles, their former self-identification—*gens de couleur libre*—no longer being a valid designation for their ethnic identity and special social status. Creole enclaves in the prairie parishes—at Palmetto, Leonville, Opelousas, Lawtell, Grand Prairie, Plaisance, Washington, Frilot Cove (Plaisance area), Rideau (Bayou Petite Prairie) and Mallet in St. Landry Parish; at Grand Marais in Iberia Parish; in and around Vermilionville in Lafayette Parish; at Grand Pointe and around St. Martinville in St. Martin

Parish; near Baldwin and along Bayou Sale in St. Mary Parish—used every means possible to preserve the social distance between themselves and their black neighbors. This is seen perhaps most clearly in the surprisingly large number of first-cousin marriages within some late nineteenth-century Creole of Color enclaves (Meyers 10–12) (Tables 12 and 13).

While discouraging social relations with the freedmen and their descendants, elders in the community simultaneously cultivated contacts with other Creole of Color communities, particularly with other prairie enclaves, but also with Creole communities in other parts of the state. "Marriages arranged by the families perpetuated the contact between the various communities. As in earlier times these marriages held the land holdings intact while also preserving the racial composition of the community" (Baker and Kreamer 87).

Some Creoles of Color also sought political involvement as a means of regaining their prewar social status. From the beginning of Reconstruction, Creoles of Color in the prairie parishes appear to have taken their new political rights and responsibilities seriously. Eight of nine "colored" jurors selected for duty in the Eighth District Court's April 27,

TABLE 12

A Demographic Profile of the Creole of Color Population
of the Attakapas and Opelousas Regions, 1870

Parish	Number	Percentage of the black population
Calcasieu	144	11.93
Cameron	85	31.84
Iberia	501	16.96
Lafayette	2,233	48.26
St. Landry	1,909	17.93
St. Martin	1,009	20.11
St. Mary	360	3.81
Vermilion	223	23.42

Source: 1870 census. The identity of the Creoles of Color enumerated in this statistical profile was based on surnames commonly known to be associated with this group.

TABLE 13

Locations of Land Transactions Involving Creoles of Color
in St. Landry Parish, Indicating Locations of
Creole of Color Enclaves

Locations	Number	Percent
Bayou Cane	1	0.55
Bayou Mallet	1	0.55
Bayou Negrofoot	1	0.55
Bayou Petite Prairie	9	4.95
Bayou Teche	6	3.30
Belaire Cove	1	0.55
Bellevue	5	2.75
Between Opelousas and Washington	4	2.20
Bois Mallet	10	5.49
Church Prairie	1	0.55
Dry Bayou	2	1.10
Grand Bois	2	1.10
Grand Prairie	6	3.30
Notleyville	6	3.30
Near Opelousas	14	7.69
Opelousas	36	19.78
Palmetto area	5	2.75
Plaisance area	24	13.19
Pointe aux Loups	1	0.55
Prairie Basse	4	2.20
Prairie Gros Chevreuil	1	0.55
Prairie Laurent	7	3.85
Prairie Mallet	7	3.85
Prairie Ronde	1	0.55
Rural unidentified	14	7.69
Tauper Flat	1	0.55
Ville Platte area	1	0.55
Washington	12	6.59
Total	182	

Source: St. Landry Parish, Conveyance Books, 1866–81.

1868, session at Opelousas, for example, were members of prominent local Creole families. Political involvement of Creoles of Color, however, was by no means limited to jury duty. The Donatos and other prominent former free men of color formed the backbone of the Republican party in the prairie parishes. These Creole politicians, who were allied politically with Governor Henry Clay Warmoth, found it expedient to portray themselves as champions of the freedmen's causes as a means of furthering their own political interests (Schweninger 352). Former free black planter Gustave Donato of St. Landry Parish, for example, was a delegate to the 1868 state constitutional convention. Other Creoles of Color held less conspicuous positions either in local government (usually the police jury and local federal patronage positions) or on party committees in the Opelousas and Attakapas areas. Creoles of Color in Opelousas, however, appear to have curtailed their political activities significantly after the bloody Opelousas riot of 1868, which claimed between twenty-five and fifty black and tan victims.

The 1868 Opelousas riot, one of the worst examples of Reconstruction violence in south Louisiana, stemmed directly from a struggle for local political hegemony. Indeed, St. Landry Parish was the scene of heated early postwar contention between Democrats and Republicans, as the rival parties sought local political domination through control of the region's large and independent black electorate. Democrats, many of whom were former Confederates, controlled most local offices in 1865 and 1866; in 1867, however, St. Landry's embryonic Republican party scored impressive electoral victories, and its slate of candidates was elected to Louisiana's 1868 constitutional convention. By mid-April 1868, however, the Democrats were able to mobilize sufficient strength to defeat ratification of the constitution within St. Landry Parish (Oubre 1973:140).

Following the Democratic victory, both parties moved to neutralize the opposition by the time of the 1868 presidential election. Some Democratic leaders organized both integrated and black-only political clubs in an effort to lure the African-American electorate into their camp. Less tolerant whites, especially former slaveholders, resorted to intimidation in an effort to force black voters into casting their ballots for the Democratic ticket (DeLatte 41–50).

Republicans were also organized into violent and nonviolent factions. The Creole of Color–led nonviolent group, evidently the larger of the two, used traditional means—rallies and barbecues—to lure voters. In their factional rallies, moderate speakers reminded freedmen that the party of Lincoln had given them freedom and warned that a Democratic presidential victory would result in their reenslavement. The violent Republicans also used political rallies as a means of disseminating their message, but instead of promoting reform by constitutional means, they openly advocated violence as a way of intimidating, and thus neutralizing, the overwhelmingly Democratic white electorate (Oubre 1973:141–42).

Incendiary admonitions of black Republican orators and the sporadic raids of Democratic night riders caused a tragic escalation of tension that eventually caused mainstream Democrats and Republicans to gravitate toward the radical elements of their respective parties and the violent remedies they advocated. Such irresponsible behavior was compounded by the increasingly acrimonious war of words between Opelousas's Democratic and Republican newspapers, particularly after the Republican police jury's December 1867 decision to award the parish printing contract to the Radical Republican organ, the *St. Landry Progress.* Citing Republican speaker Sam Johnson's admonition to disband black Democrats at the "point of the bayonet or, if necessary, by burning the town [of Washington]," James W. Jackson, editor of the *Opelousas Journal,* called upon his fellow Democrats to take a forceful stand, lest the Louisiana Republicans turn every local Democratic official out of office.

> White men of St. Landry, see that your shot guns, rifles and six shooters are in good condition. The negroes, driven on by the carpetbaggers and scalawags among us, are continually talking about their guns; and the valiant Sam Johnson says what they lack in guns, they will make up in matches. . . .
>
> Then beware, white men. An ounce of prevention is better than a pound of cure. So we say again, keep your guns in order. Keep plenty of buckshot and powder on hand. Act on the defensive but if forced to move, move like a whirlwind and sweep everything before you. (*Opelousas Journal,* September 12, 1868)

Such inflammatory exhortations produced a predictable response: a direct confrontation between armed groups of Democrats and Republicans near Washington in late September that nearly erupted into a riot. Violence was averted temporarily when leaders of the opposing camps negotiated a political truce, but the truce was broken on September 28, when a local judge inflicted a severe caning upon Emerson Bently, the white Radical editor of the *Progress* and teacher in a black school. Fleeing in the midst of the resulting confusion, some of the schoolchildren mistakenly informed their parents that Bently and some of the black children in the school had been murdered. The parents sent distress signals to local Republican leaders, including Creoles of Color, who, in turn, dispatched couriers throughout the parish calling for full mobilization of armed supporters to assemble at Opelousas. Among these messengers was a courier dispatched by Gustave Donato, a member of the St. Landry Republican Executive Committee, to Sam Johnson (Oubre 1973:146–47).

This call to arms, initially made by a white Republican, was unsuccessfully opposed by several prominent blacks, including Creole of Color Cornelius Donato, who hoped to avoid an armed confrontation between the races. These fears were quickly realized. By noon on the twenty-eighth, armed bands of blacks approached Opelousas from the west, east, and south. Alarmed by news of the impending invasion, Opelousas's municipal officials sounded an alarm and organized a posse to pacify the rural area surrounding the parish seat. Meanwhile, black politicians from Opelousas went into the countryside to refute rumors of Bently's death and to persuade incoming blacks to return home. These Opelousas representatives were initially successful, and the posse encountered no resistance in the immediate vicinity of Opelousas. Along the Bellevue Road, south of Opelousas, however, the posse encountered Creole of Color H. S. Frilot, a parish police juror, and disarmed him. With Frilot in their custody, the posse then moved south, along the Bellevue Road, until they encountered Creole of Color Hilaire Paillet (Oubre 1973:147–48).

Paillet complained that his farm had been occupied by a band of armed blacks. He said that Creole of Color Adolphe Donato, returning home from Opelousas, had informed the occupiers that Bently had been beaten, not killed, and that no children were injured, that it was a private matter, and that blacks should not become involved. Donato's appeal for calm was met with contempt by his audience, who called for the murder of a local white man. Donato and Paillet had then departed, the latter in search of help (Oubre 1973:148).

Upon encountering Paillet, the posse proceeded directly to his farm. Following a call to disarm, firing commenced and continued until a cease-fire was arranged by Frilot to permit the evacuation of women and children from the Paillet house. The twenty-five black resisters subsequently surrendered and were escorted to the parish jail by the posse (Oubre 1973:148–49).

The armed confrontation at Paillet's farm sparked a full-fledged race riot. On the night of September 28, armed blacks from Bois Mallet killed a white man attempting to join armed bands of whites then gathering in the Opelousas area. Whites attempted to assassinate François D'Avy, a white man largely responsible for the Republican call to arms (Oubre 1973:149).

The following day, approximately two thousand armed whites converged on Opelousas. Bands of whites then disarmed all blacks within a twenty-five-mile radius of Opelousas, killing any who attempted to resist, while other invaders destroyed the presses of the *St. Landry Progress*. That night, the vigilantes removed the prisoners arrested at Paillet's from the parish jail, took them out of Opelousas, and then executed them, along with one of the *Progress*'s white editors (Oubre 1973: 149–50).

The death toll from these activities varies tremendously depending on the source. Democratic accounts maintain that two whites were killed and four wounded and that black casualties amounted to five killed and one wounded. An independent military investigation estimated that twenty-five blacks had died in the "riot." Republican sources, however, placed the black death toll at two hundred to three hundred. There is unanimity regarding the outcome of the disturbance, stated best perhaps by the following contemporary account from the October 10, 1868, issue of the pro-Democratic *Franklin Planters' Banner*:

> The negroes all over the Parish have been disarmed, and have gone to work briskly. Their loyal league clubs have been broken up, the scallawags have turned Democrats, and the carpet-baggers have run off, and their carpet-bag press and type and office have been destroyed. St. Landry is quiet for the first time since the War.

The people generally are well satisfied with the result of the St. Landry riot, only they regret that the Carpet-Baggers escaped. The editor escaped; and a hundred dead negroes, and perhaps a hundred more wounded and crippled, a dead white Radical, a dead Democrat, and three or four wounded Democrats are the upshot of the business.

As the *Planters' Banner* suggests, white Democrats maintained a virtual reign of terror in the wake of the uprising. In the days following the riot, only blacks wearing a red arm band indicating that they had surrendered and were seeking white protection were safe from the vigilante onslaught (DeLatte 47–50).

The precipitous constriction of black civil rights produced a corresponding diminution of black political power. In fact, the Republican party virtually ceased to exist in St. Landry Parish after 1868. By the early 1870s, many prominent St. Landry Republicans had become Democrats, including members of the Donato clan (U.S. House of Representatives 164). Even as late as 1876, however, Creoles of Color Adolphe Donato and Napoleon Lastrapes of St. Landry Parish waged strong but unsuccessful campaigns for state representative, garnering 1,738 and 2,011 votes respectively in their home parish (*Opelousas Courier*, November 18, 1876). Creole politicians remained active in other areas of the prairie country until the end of Reconstruction, and several were elected to the state legislature.

CHAPTER SIX

Conclusion

Throughout the colonial and antebellum periods, the Creoles of Color had existed as a separate class, distinct from the dominant whites as well as from the slaves. Although they did not enjoy full citizenship rights and privileges, they did have considerably more rights and privileges than the servile population. During the Civil War, as portions of the state came under Union control, the *gens de couleur libre* attempted to maintain the three-tier social system that guaranteed them separate status. Union officials, however, were unwilling to recognize this distinction and insisted on treating all persons of African ancestry as members of a single class. This monolithic view of nonwhites was institutionalized by the black codes that followed the war's end.

Once they accepted the realities of their new situation, the Creoles of Color determined that if they were to be classed with the freedmen they would be the social and political leaders of their race (Vincent 17). They reasoned that because they had experienced the problems of being free in a white man's world, were educated, and were property owners, they had earned the right to leadership. It is hardly surprising, then, that the Creoles of Color, who constituted a small minority of the African-American population in south-central Louisiana, occupied a disproportionately large number of political positions and wielded a disproportionately large amount of political influence in the Reconstruction era. All of the black representatives from the prairie region to the 1868 state constitutional convention were Creoles of Color: Auguste Donato, Jr., St. Landry Parish; Fortuné Riard, Lafayette Parish; Sosthene Snaer, St. Martin Parish; Jean-Baptiste Esnard, St. Mary Parish.

Creoles of Color also supplied half the black state legislators and all of the black state senators to represent St. Landry, Lafayette, St. Martin, and St. Mary parishes during Reconstruction: representatives Jean-Baptiste Esnard (1868–72), L. A. Martinet (1874–75), and Victor Rochon (1872–75); Arthur Antoine (1872–74) and senators Alexandre François (1868–May 1869) and Emile Detiège (1874–76) (Vincent 148, 226–37).

Creole of Color politicians, however, could maintain themselves in power only if they effectively promoted the interests of their black constituents. In many areas, the interests of these fledgling politicians coincided with those of their formerly enslaved constituents. One area of major concern to both groups was the legitimacy of marriages and children. During the antebellum and Civil War eras, slave marriages were not recognized, nor were the interracial unions that many Creoles of Color had entered. Therefore, one of the first bills introduced by the 1868 legislature was "An Act Relative to Marriage." The first provision of the act validated all private or religious marriages contracted before the act's passage. The second section provided for the legitimization of all children born of those unions. Another section legalized interracial unions and one provided a means whereby common-law marriages could be legalized (Vincent 102–3). Although this act was ostensibly aimed at correcting the problems created by slavery, it also served the needs of the Creoles of Color, especially the provision legalizing interracial marriages and common-law liaisons. The bill was passed in November 1868 and went into effect immediately.

To assure the legitimacy of children born of slave unions, Representative Robert Isabelle, a Creole of Color and a native of Opelousas (Vincent 55), introduced bills in both the 1868 and 1870 legislative sessions. The 1870 "Act to Authorize Natural Parents to Legitimate Their Natural Children" provided that natural fathers and mothers who had been prevented from legitimizing their children because of antebellum laws could now accomplish this merely by declaring their intention before a notary public and two witnesses (Vincent 103). Again, although this act was aimed primarily at providing legitimacy for children born to slave parents, it also made it possible for Creoles of Color and their white partners to legitimize their progeny.

Creoles of Color and their black constituents also found common ground in the areas of voting, political rights, and, especially, desegregation of public facilities. Once again, Isabelle assumed the mantle of leadership in the Louisiana legislature's attempt to grant persons of African-American background equal access to public carriers and accommodations. On July 10, 1868, the Radical Republican submitted to the Louisiana General Assembly a bill barring racial discrimination in public transportation, business, and public accommodations. Violators were subject to mandatory fines up to $100 or one year's imprisonment. Both houses of the legislature quickly approved the civil rights measure and, in September 1868, sent it to Governor Henry Clay Warmoth for his approval. Fearing that the "coercive" legislation would spark racial unrest, however, Warmoth vetoed the desegregation bill (Fischer 64–66).

Warmoth's veto elicited an immediate outburst from the legislature. Isabelle, in a speech that belied his personal biases regarding phenotype and social rank, publicly condemned the existing segregation system that equated Mexicans and olive-skinned Europeans with whites but denied persons of African-American descent "all the rights and privileges of the white man" (Fischer 64–66).

Galvanized by such rhetoric, the black members of the state legislature resolved to reintroduce Isabelle's desegregation bill but in a slightly modified form more palatable to whites. The new civil rights bill required open admission to all public facilities, but it provided specific conditions under which patrons of any race could legally be refused service at public establishments (e.g., chronic nonpayment of bills, disorderly conduct). Victims of discrimination could sue business proprietors for damages. The bill cleared the house and senate the following February, and it was signed by a reluctant Warmoth on February 23, 1869 (Fischer 67–90).

Because most blacks lacked the financial means to bring suit against violators of the 1869 civil rights act, many white businessmen openly defied its ban on racial discrimination. Representative Isabelle attempted to solve the problem of enforcement by introducing legislation restoring criminal penalties—particularly fines—for civil rights infractions. The bill passed the house on March 9, 1870, and the senate three days later. But Warmoth, now a vocal opponent of desegregation, held the bill on his desk until January 2, 1871, when he vetoed it.

Because of his notable contributions to the postbellum civil rights crusade, Robert Isabelle's political career easily overshadowed those of other Creole of Color legislators originally from, or actually representing, the prairie region. Their lackluster performance in the legislature was undoubtedly owing, in part, to the violent nature of contemporary Louisiana politics and the constant threat of violence that attended overt support of black civil and political rights, as promising young Senator Alexandre François discovered at the cost of his life. François, a former free man of color from St. Martin Parish, where he had been a butcher, merchant, and planter, served in the 1868 state constitutional convention before being elected the same year to the state senate. François's senatorial career was short-lived, however. In May 1869, shortly after his election, he was confronted and beaten severely by members of a politically prominent family to whom he had publicly attributed all the area's ills during the campaign. François died of his injuries approximately three weeks later (Vincent 75–201).

It should hardly be surprising that local Creole of Color politicians subsequently maintained a low public profile, although they courageously supported civil rights legislation introduced by legislators from other areas of the state. Such support involved more than a small element of personal risk at a time of heightened racial tensions. The only noteworthy piece of legislation introduced by prairie area Creoles of Color was an 1873 bill by Representative Rochon allowing St. Martinville blacks to incorporate their own Catholic church (Vincent 75–201).

Creoles of Color from the prairie parishes remained politically active throughout Reconstruction. With the end of Reconstruction, they were unable to win election to the legislature, though Creoles of Color from other portions of the state continued to serve in the state senate. Prairie Creoles of Color, however, supported their confrères in the legislature, who consistently fought to expand and maintain the Reconstruction gains made toward political and social parity with whites. This valiant civil and political rights campaign was successful until 1890; then, as the political influence of Creoles of Color slowly waned, the Bourbon Redeemers gradually began to remove the social gains they had fought so hard to earn and maintain. In 1890, the legislature passed Act 111, which established separate accommodations for whites and blacks on trolleys and railroad cars and forbade blacks from attempting to occupy seats in the cars reserved for whites. The Creoles of Color in New Orleans, with financial support from those in the prairie parishes and Natchitoches, decided to challenge the law. A newly organized citizens committee selected Daniel Desdunes to test the interstate aspects of the law. They were successful in this endeavor. The committee tapped Homère Plessy to challenge the law's intrastate provisions. Although the Creole of Color plaintiffs lost in state court, the committee determined to appeal the decision to the United States Supreme Court (Desdunes 1973: 141–44). Albion W. Tourgée, who prepared the committee's brief for the Supreme Court, argued that "the reputation of belonging to the dominant race, in this instance the white race, is *property* . . . and that the provisions of the act in question which authorize an officer of a railroad company to assign a person to a car set apart for a particular race, enables such officer to deprive him, to a certain extent at least, of this property—this reputation which has an actual pecuniary value— 'without due process of law,' and are therefore a violation of the Second restrictive clause of the first section of the XIVth Amendment" (Olsen 83). He further argued that "the crime, then, for which he became liable to imprisonment . . . was that a person of seven-eights Caucasian blood insisted in sitting peacefully and quietly in a car the state of Louisiana had commanded the company to set aside exclusively for the white race. . . . Will the court hold that a single drop of African blood is sufficient to color a whole ocean of Caucasian whiteness?" His major argument then became not whether the facilities were equal but "the right of the state to label one citizen as white and another as colored in the common enjoyment of a public . . . railway" (Olsen 98).

Having failed in *Plessy* v. *Ferguson,* Louisiana's Creoles of Color chose not to challenge a subsequent law that forbade interracial marriages (Desdunes 1973:145). Then, in 1898, the community's remaining political rights were completely extinguished by the new white supremacist state constitution. At the dawn of the twentieth century, Creoles of Color in the prairie parishes found themselves with little more than their lands, their pride, and their ethnic identity. Yet these were enough to sustain them and to propel them into the new century.

Many Creoles of Color who had scaled the economic heights of the boom period of the 1840s and 1850s had great difficulty in dealing with the depths of the postbellum depression. They looked back nostalgically to the antebellum period, which, like former white planters, they came to regard as something of a golden age. Again, like former white slaveholders, some economic casualties of the war never fully came to terms with the loss of their world. Adolphe Donato's postwar existence provides a poignant epitaph for these individuals.

In 1883, Adolphe Donato, "a member of one of the richest black slave-owning families in the South," was working as a body servant to a white man. Accompanying his employer to the nation's capital, he saw streets "as smooth as glass" and buildings "more magnificent than I ever dreamed of." "My room is small but I have a good bed and a stove and, what is better than anything else, a servant comes in every morning to make my fire." Just think, he explained to a friend in Opelousas, how much of a luxury it was to be waited on, "but then you Know folks of fashion are bound to put on airs." Dressing in the latest style, strolling along Pennsylvania Avenue, window shopping at the downtown stores, he feigned being a "distinguished colored gentleman." Each morning, however, he was expected to serve his employer coffee and then wash the cups and saucers. "But I do this so quietly," he noted, "that the servant never supposes for a moment that I am other than a 'gentleman of leisure'" (Schweninger 359).

Ironically, just when it appeared that the entire nation had turned its back on the plight of southern blacks, Congress allowed former Creole of Color property owners to file suit with the Court of Claims for destruction of property by the Union forces during the Civil War. As a representative of the heirs of Auguste Donato, Cornelius Donato requested on July 9, 1897, that the Probate Court of St. Landry Parish allow him to post a bond of $7,500 so that he could file suit for the loss of $58,500. When the Court of Claims finally acted in 1905, it awarded the Donato heirs a settlement of $12,570 (St. Landry Parish, Probate 3766).

Other members of the prairie Creole of Color community proved more resilient than Adolphe Donato. Indeed, as noted in Chapter 5 and documented in Appendix B, Creoles of Color remained surprisingly active economically until sometime in the 1880s, engaging in a disproportionately large number of land transactions. Many of these transactions were between Creoles of Color, suggesting attempts to consolidate or enlarge familial landholdings.

These myriad conveyance records indicate that by the end of Reconstruction, several Creole of Color families had established distinct communities throughout the prairie country, including Prairie Laurent near Leonville; at Rideau, near Palmetto; at Frilot Cove, near Plaisance; at Mallet, near Eunice; and at Anse de Prien Noir, Rougon, and Soileau in what would later become Evangeline Parish (Spitzer 54).

Denizens of these communities clearly hoped that their physical isolation and exclusive landownership within the settlements would help them preserve their identity, culture, racial integrity, and elevated social status within African-American society. Writing in 1866 for *Harper's New Monthly Magazine,* Nathan Willey maintained that "these people have little to do with the Freedmen's Bureau, and do not recognize it as having any application to themselves. They object to being placed in the same class with the freedmen just released from bondage, and seem to feel that they are a superior race, in the enjoyment of advantages which their less fortunate neighbors never obtained. . . . They as firmly believe that the inferiority of condition necessarily attaches to itself a lasting dishonor as the whites do that color is a badge of inferior race." As before the war, "the Creoles of Color continued to use the term [Creole] and also hold themselves above the blacks, including those French-speakers who had been slaves on French plantations" (Spitzer 58). Indeed, extant coroners' inquests for the period 1885–1900 indicate that many St. Landry Creoles of Color continued to apply the even more archaic term "free person of color" to themselves well into the twilight days of the nineteenth century as a means of distinguishing themselves from local freedmen and their descendants.

The perceived need for such exclusiveness grew as the socioeconomic and cultural gaps narrowed between the Creoles of Color and other local African-Americans. The 1910 federal census indicates that the markers traditionally used to distinguish Creoles from their postbellum black neighbors—skin color, wealth, landownership, education, and language—were no longer sufficiently different to divide the two populations on their own merits. This is particularly true of the ascriptive differences between Creoles of Color and the non-Creole but French-speaking and Catholic minority in the region's larger African-American population. Demographic profiles of the latter group—whose descendants have, since 1980, come to identify themselves as "black Creoles"—and the well-established Creole of Color communities were

virtually indistinguishable. With the notable exception of St. Landry Parish, where 56 percent of all black Creoles were dark-complected African-Americans, both groups were overwhelmingly mulatto (light-complected): Creoles of Color—60 percent in Wards 1–3 of St. Landry Parish; 70 percent in Ward 1 of St. Martin Parish; 77.81 percent in Ward 1 of Lafayette Parish; black Creoles—66 percent in Ward 1 of St. Martin Parish; 88.57 percent in Ward 1 of Lafayette Parish. This similarity in phenotype suggests that many, if not most, black Creoles were—like the Creoles of Color—descendants of the natural children of whites, whose surnames they had adopted after the Civil War, and their slave concubines, but, unlike the Creoles of Color, their ancestors had remained in bondage until the end of slavery.

There were equally striking economic parallels between the two groups as a result of the protracted decline in the collective fortunes of the Creole of Color community. In both groups, a majority of households rented the farms the enumerated families cultivated, though the tendency toward tenantry was slightly more pronounced in the black Creole group: Creoles of Color—68 percent in Wards 1–3 of St. Landry Parish; 54 percent in Ward 1 of St. Martin Parish; black Creoles—86 percent in Wards 1–3 of St. Landry Parish; 56 percent in Ward 1 of St. Martin Parish.

The declining economic fortunes of the Creoles of Color had also helped close the educational gap between them and black Creoles. Before and during the Civil War, Creole of Color children—particularly in the Washington area of St. Landry Parish—generally enjoyed a higher level of literacy than their counterparts in the Cajun and white Creole communities, whereas the enslaved progenitors of the black Creole group were almost universally illiterate. The impoverishment of many Creole of Color families in the late nineteenth century made education an expensive luxury, particularly after yeomen were reduced to tenantry. By 1910, few members of either group were able either to read and write or to send their children to school. In St. Landry and St. Martin parishes, however, school attendance among Creole of Color children was slightly more common. The 1910 federal census indicates that only 16 percent of all Creoles of Color in Wards 1–3 were literate, while only 14 percent of all school-aged Creole of Color children attended school. But no Creole of Color children attended school in Ward 2 of Acadia Parish in 1910, while 6.61 percent of all children in the region's African-American community as a whole attended classes for at least part of the school year.

Only in the area of linguistics was there a notable difference between the two groups. Like the white elite in the prairie parishes, the most affluent Creoles of Color had for a generation felt mounting pressure for cultural and linguistic assimilation into the American "mainstream" resulting from the national Progressive movement. As in the white community, the elite gradually abandoned French for English. In the 1910 population schedules, fully 59 percent of all Creoles of Color in Wards 1–3 of St. Landry Parish spoke English, while in Ward 1 of St. Martin Parish, only a bare majority (54 percent) of all Creoles of Color spoke their traditional mother tongue. In Ward 2 of Acadia Parish, only two of seventy-two resident Creoles of Color spoke French. But French remained the dominant language of the black Creoles: 62 percent of all black Creoles in Wards 1–3 of St. Landry Parish as well as in Ward 1 of St. Martin Parish spoke French as their first language.

The narrowing of the cultural and economic gulfs traditionally separating Creoles of Color from their neighbors heightened the siege mentality already present within the Creole of Color community. This situation was exacerbated still further by the intermarriage of several poor Creole of Color women to dark-skinned French-speaking black Creoles in St. Landry and St. Martin parishes in the early decades of the twentieth century (1910 census). In an effort to prevent their own children from also marrying beneath their social station, elders of several Creole of Color settlements imposed increasingly stringent—sometimes draconian—measures to reduce contact with outsiders.

The Creoles' attempts to distance themselves from the former freedmen and their descendants took many forms. One contemporary observer reported that in the wake of the Civil War, prosperous Creoles of Color sent their children to the fifteen or sixteen exclusive Creole of Color schools in New Orleans (Willey 247–48), scrupulously avoiding the region's new public schools, which had become the exclusive domain of former slave children (Fischer 96–97, 101, 103). Normal tensions between Creole of Color landlords and their black sharecropper employees also helped both to maintain class distinctions and to discourage fraternization between the two groups. Other attempts to diminish contact with the freedmen were far less subtle, involving overt Creole attempts to exclude blacks from social gatherings. The oral traditions of both the Creole of Color and black communities contain repeated references to the so-called paper-bag test applied by "bouncers" to individuals wishing to enter Creole of Color dances or socials. "This involved the comparison of a person of questionable phenotype"—a person of dark skin color—"with a paper bag. If he was the shade of the bag or lighter, he could enter the club or other social function." A few informants also maintain that the "bouncers" also subjected suspected black patrons to a second, more humiliating examination called the "comb test." If a person's hair was sufficiently straight to permit a comb to run through it, he could, in the words of one observer, "zydeco all night" (Spitzer 58).

Such restrictive tests were double-edged swords for, though they were effective in limiting access to members of the sponsoring community, they also effectively limited the pool of potential spouses to relatives belonging to the community. To avoid the problems associated with consanguineous marriages, the elders of the various communities continued to arrange marriages for their children with members of other Creole of Color communities within the parish and elsewhere in the state; consequently, familial networks frequently stretched from the prairies "through New Roads, Marksville right up through Alexandria to the Cane River, from Melrose right into Natchitoches." The intent of these alliances was to preserve the racial composition of the community and to maintain the family's economic status (Spitzer 111–12; Baker and Kreamer 87).

Such efforts were initially successful, but after 1880, succeeding generations were either financially unable or simply unwilling to expand or even maintain familial landholdings in the various Creole of Color communities. Consequently, many large plantations, when divided among numerous heirs, soon devolved into compact clusters of small farms, thereby creating densely populated and tightly knit communities that gradually acquired their own identities. Because of Louisiana's forced heirship laws, the size of individual landholdings was inexorably reduced with each succeeding generation, and by World War II many families that had once been wealthy were fortunate to maintain more than a subsistence existence.

Though they had lost their wealth, the Creoles of Color had not lost either their unique social status or their pride. The social mechanisms put into place during the postbellum era to insulate the former free people of color from the freedmen persisted in the prairie communities at least until the 1940s; indeed, they appear to have been intensified in the early twentieth century as mounting segregationist pressures threatened to draw the Creole of Color community fully into the state's maturing biracial society. One could argue that in the 1940s, despite the cumulative effect of decades of segregation, Creole of Color society was little different from that of the 1880s. In the words of one informant, "The whites wouldn't accept us, and the blacks fought us because we looked like whites" (Spitzer 119).

The community's continuing intermediate social and racial status was first subjected to scholarly scrutiny after World War II. In 1949, Louisiana State University sociology student Joseph H. Jones studied one of the prairie enclaves of Creoles of Color, Frilot Cove. His master's thesis provides a microcosmic view of how these proud people fared in the first half of the twentieth century (Jones 20–40). Oral tradition in Frilot Cove holds that the community was founded during the latter part of the antebellum period by Pierre Elisio Frilot, Edouard Fusilier, Philogene Auzenne, and Phillipe Frilot, all Creoles of Color who had moved from the Prairie Laurent area (Jones 28). In 1929, seventeen men were listed as property owners within the community with total acreage of 1,671 and average landholding of 98 acres. By 1949 the number of property owners had more than doubled, but the average acreage had fallen to less than one-third the 1929 level. In 1949 the community consisted of fifty families whose primary occupation was agriculture, although they supplemented their income through carpentry, work in the building trades, and employment in the heavy industries at Lake Charles and Baton Rouge (Jones 36–38).

The community of Frilot Cove in 1949 was 1,400 acres in size (a little more than two square miles) with a population of 302 residents. The population density was 137.5 persons per square mile, nearly twice that of the surrounding area of St. Landry Parish, which was 76.9 persons per square mile. This made for a very tight-knit community, and although one would assume that such density would signify poverty, the opposite was the case. The average number of rooms in the houses in Frilot Cove was 5.8 while only 14.5 percent of all dwellings in the entire parish of St. Landry had more than 5 rooms (Jones 42). The major criticism the 1950 generation had of the founders was that they failed to buy more land when it was inexpensive and readily available. As a result, many children had to leave the community because there was no land left for them (Jones 53).

Frilot Cove's waxing economic fortunes mirrored those of the larger Creole of Color community as a whole. In the early to mid-twentieth century, hundreds of prairie Creoles sought a better life in the Golden Triangle area of southeastern Texas; at Oakland, Richmond, Torrance, or Simi Valley, California; or in the industrial centers of the Midwest, particularly Chicago (Tenney interview). These transplanted farmers and ranchers found better economic opportunities in their adopted homes, but economic advancement came at the cost of new challenges to their traditional identity as they adapted to alien and sometimes hostile environments. Threatened by assimilation into the larger black community, these Creoles of Color, like their late nineteenth-century ancestors, drew in among themselves, establishing tightly knit communities that have survived to the present through endogamy. In an analysis of one transplanted community in the late 1970s, Sister Frances Jerome Woods discovered that 67.7 percent of all marriages involving these prairie country expatriates were Creole-to-Creole unions; 21.0 percent were unions between Creoles of Color and blacks; and 11.3 percent were between Creoles of Color and whites. Such self-imposed insularity has allowed the transplanted culture not only to survive but to flourish. The Los Angeles–area Creole community publishes a cultural newsletter, *Bayou Talk,* with a national circulation of approximately six thousand. The southern California group also sponsors regular cultural festivals. The northern California community for decades has imported zydeco musicians from southwestern Louisiana (Woods 1972: 59–61, 76).

Sustained contacts between mother and daughter cultures have helped the expatriates to remain abreast of the staggering changes occurring in Louisiana over the past five decades. Fundamental economic changes, which began during World War II, have continued to the present. The war gave a major economic boost to such communities as Frilot Cove, which provided laborers and skilled craftsmen for construction of Camps Claiborne, Livingston, and Polk. Following construction of the training camps, Creoles of Color from Frilot Cove helped build the massive Cities Service oil refinery in Lake Charles, Louisiana. Farmers and ranchers from the prairie communities participated in these construction projects on a seasonal basis, tending their crops for six months and working in the building trades the remainder of the year. When engaged in construction work, the men from Frilot Cove and other communities commuted daily to building sites 60 to 120 miles away, leaving home around 4:00 A.M. and returning around 8:00 P.M. (Jones 115–16).

These strenuous daily commutes bear silent testimony to the tremendous emphasis on family and family values, which remain cultural hallmarks of the Creole of Color community. In the late 1940s, adult residents of Frilot Cove were justly proud of the values they shared and had instilled in their children. They pointed with pride to the fact that no one from the community had ever been arrested, even for speeding, and that only one marriage had ended in separation. They also noted proudly that their children were industrious, thrifty, and deferential, with a keen appreciation of their families, their culture, and their heritage (Jones 171–77).

The Frilot Cove elders also pointed with pride to their children's acceptance of their religious heritage. Prairie Creoles of Color have long been known for the strength of their religious values. Although "Creole women are far more numerous than men in formal participation in the church," reflecting the anticlerical biases of the region's "French peasantry who viewed the Church as a colonial European institution run by non-locals and the literate upper class," an abiding devotion to the Catholic faith persists among Creoles of Color (Spitzer 247–48). They have constituted the backbone of the largest group of rural black Catholics in the United States for the past two centuries and have furnished a surprisingly large number of priests and religious in the late twentieth century, including four prelates.

The Creole of Color emphasis on Catholicism (as well as folk Catholicism and the use of *traiteurs*, faith healers), family (both nuclear and extended), family values, and hard work mirror the values of neighboring Cajun and white Creole communities, with whom they also shared a common language (Spitzer viii). The strain of French spoken by rural Creoles of Color is Cajun French, whereas New Orleans's Creoles of Color, like their white Creole counterparts, speak standard French (Dominguez 1979:226). This common cultural, linguistic, and religious base has provided a basis for extensive cross-cultural borrowing over the last century: "People of Afro- and French descent, whether they call themselves Creoles, Creoles of Color, or black Creoles (as is now common), share to a large degree the language, religion, foodways, material culture, music, dance, and festival styles of Cajuns. However, many of these elements of Cajun culture have been profoundly influenced by the black Creoles. While there is a good deal of cultural overlap between Cajuns and black Creoles there is also a clear social separation in many domains" (Spitzer 61).

This separation is perhaps most evident in the development of Cajun and zydeco (black Creole) music since the onset of the local music recording industry in the 1920s. Cajun and zydeco music developed from two distinct musical traditions drawn respectively from France and West Africa, but as neighboring Cajun and black Creole sharecroppers began to play music together in the early part of this century and, after the late 1920s, to listen to one another's recordings, each began to borrow tunes and musical styles from the other. As a result of these exchanges, both Cajun and zydeco music were fundamentally transformed. The leading authority on zydeco notes that

> Zydeco is the traditional dance music of black Creoles in rural Louisiana. It is played at a variety of settings including house parties, church fairs, church halls, community benefit dances, bars and dance halls. Zydeco, like black French culture in general, represents a creolization of influences from African, Afro-French West Indian, Afro-American and Acadian cultures. Musically zydeco is a mixture of Cajun dance songs (tunes, texts, rhythms), Afro-American blues (tunes, texts, tonality) and Afro-Caribbean rhythms. According to most musicians, the term zydeco (considered in folk etymology as a creolization of *les haricots*, "snapbeans") refers to the fast syncopated two-steps in every group's repertoire. Though the song titles and texts are often the same as Cajun music, these numbers are distinguished as black Creole by their syncopated rhythms and staccato melodic lines built around call-response voicings. (Spitzer 300)

Ethnomusicologist Barry Jean Ancelet is more specific:

> European song tradition tended to be textually oriented. Ballads and folksongs were traditionally unaccompanied and sung for their content. In African tradition, music, singing and dancing were all inextricably related and this may have influenced the combination of singing and instrumental traditions. . . . The result of this process . . . was the development of new songs which combined the two traditions. (Ancelet 19)
> "Les Barres de la prison," Canray Fontenot's classic blues waltz based on Douglas Bellard's original recording of "La Valse de la prison," for example, is a traditional gallows blues lament or prisoner's farewell which recalls the old French "Chanson de Mandrin." (Ancelet 22)

The independent but parallel development of Cajun and zydeco continued apace throughout the twentieth century, but by the 1980s, young musicians in both musical camps shared a large, common repertoire of songs from both traditions, played in virtually identical styles.

The culturally syncretic process that linked the Cajun and Creole of Color communities was less evident between the Creole of Color and black communities, at least until after World War II. In the late 1940s and early 1950s, the Creoles of Color remained a marginal group trapped between the dominant white and minority black societies, and prevailing customs and attitudes helped reinforce the black Creoles' marginal status. In the late 1940s, older members of the Frilot Cove community reportedly forbade their children to associate with anyone darker than they (Jones 178).

It was impossible for Creole of Color children to adhere scrupulously to their parents' admonitions, for Louisiana's compulsory education and segregation laws forced those who were unable to afford private education to attend school with black children. The groups' mutual animosities led initially to clashes, which paradoxically forced the combatants to see one another in a new light. One participant recalled "goin' to school [in the 1940s] with the darker skinned Negroes, that they looked upon us as sort of inferior because our skin was lighter than theirs. Because of this we got into a lot of fights, but we protected our honor and eventually we got along good together" (quoted in Spitzer 119).

A sociological study of the Frilot Cove community noted that young adults respected their parents' cultural mores as long as they were in the prairie community but that those who had served in the military, had helped build the military training camps, had attended college—particularly Southern University in Baton Rouge and Xavier University in New Orleans—had begun to forge personal relationships with blacks of lower social status (Jones 178).

The traditional barriers between the Creoles of Color and blacks began to crumble when both groups entered the civil rights movement in the 1950s and 1960s. Throughout the twentieth century, prairie Creoles of Color were torn between conflicting pressures—those from within the community to gravitate toward the French-speaking white population and those from outside exerted by the French-speaking white community itself to be black. As Nicholas Spitzer has noted

> Increasingly in the second quarter of the 20th century, Creole people opted to be black. In moving towards a black mainstream . . . many black Creoles went beyond cultural traits to physical extremes that today seem odd. For example, in the 1950s and 1960s when some blacks in America were straightening or "conking" their hair and using skin lighteners as a

result of aesthetics and values projected by white Madison Avenue, light-skinned Louisiana Creoles were actually trying to be blacker. . . . Louisiana's young black Creoles of the 1950s and 1960s, whose parents had tried for many years to be either white, or at least a European-affiliated, Afro-French group unto themselves, were now going in the opposite direction—often to the horror of elders—and trying consciously to be black. (Spitzer 128–29)

This change in racial and cultural affiliation was coupled with a corresponding increase in Creole of Color marriages to black Creoles or English-speaking African-Americans.

This metamorphosis led to a blurring of the traditional distinction between Creoles of Color and the French- and Creole-speaking descendants of slaves, who in the 1980s began to refer to themselves as black Creoles, thereby further clouding the issue of identity within the Creole of Color community, and with English-speaking blacks who constitute a majority of south Louisiana's African-American population. This rapprochement between the Creole of Color community and the black underclass paved the way for the establishment of an effective civil rights movement on the local and regional levels in the prairie country. In joining the civil rights movement, Creoles of Color heeded the admonition fellow Creole Rodolphe Desdunes had addressed to W. E. B. Du Bois in 1907. Rejecting Du Bois's call for domination of the Negro race by the talented tenth, Desdunes insisted that "by striving for justice, justice we may obtain, [but] by reaching out for justice and domination, we are in danger of losing both" (Desdunes 1973:14). Both groups found strength in unity, and this alliance permitted the former adversaries to bridge the chasm between their societies. Together, they won the right to vote in the 1950s, and, together once again, as they had during Reconstruction, they led the fight for universal civil rights. On January 8, 1954, two Creoles of Color and two non-Creole blacks from south-central Louisiana filed suit against Southwestern Louisiana Institute (present-day University of Southwestern Louisiana) alleging that the Lafayette college had refused to enroll African-Americans "without due process of law." On May 17, a federal judicial panel ordered the school to integrate, and the following July 22, John Harold Taylor of Arnaudville, Louisiana, registered in the school's engineering program without incident. By the end of the 1954–55 school session, seventy-five blacks—most of them Creoles of Color—had enrolled. Southwestern Louisiana Institute had become the first white institution of higher learning in the South to integrate (Brasseaux 1990:31).

Their leadership role in the civil rights movement positioned the Creoles of Color to serve, once again, as the leadership element of the black community when political and voting rights were at long last restored. Creoles of Color constitute a disproportionately large percentage of all black officeholders in the prairie country (Louisiana, *Roster of Officials*, 1973–93).

But not all members of the Creole of Color community have been completely comfortable with the group's political and cultural alliance with the non-Creole black community; nor indeed have some blacks accepted the Creoles of Color, as is evident in the continuing sporadic clashes between dark- and light-skinned blacks in south Louisiana's public school yards. Creoles of Color most sensitive to the question of race, particularly among those persons aspiring to full acceptance by the local white society, have been wrangling with the legal basis for racial identification for generations. For these individuals, who constitute a significant but as yet undetermined portion of the Creole of Color community, racial identification is a problem that remains unresolved because they have not become fully reconciled to the group leadership's political rapprochement with the black community. Such continuing alienation is, in large part, a legacy of the tripartite organization of lower Mississippi Valley society—whites, persons of mixed racial background, and blacks—in which class and status was an overriding concern of everyday life.

In rural southwestern Louisiana, racial identification for many Creoles of Color was ultimately a question of social status, grounded in the peculiar circumstances of the region's development. The French colonists who clustered along the lower Mississippi River and Gulf Coast in the early eighteenth century attempted to recreate in the New World a romanticized version of the old, with themselves as the aristocracy. Their preoccupation with class led to the creation of complex and rigid social stratification in colonial society, vestiges of which have survived to the present in Gulf Coast society. The boundary between racial groups—white, tan, and black—was ultimately a class boundary. Within the Creole of Color community itself, however, social rank was often based as much on skin color as on economic status. In describing class consciousness in antebellum Louisiana's free black society, historian Annie Stahl, who borrowed heavily from Willey's nineteenth-century observations, noted that "free colored people believed that the inferiority of condition necessarily attached to itself a lasting dishonor as the whites believed that color was a badge of an inferior race. . . . The standard of respectability among free people of color contained many gradations of color" (360).

Eyewitness accounts indicate that by the time of the Civil War, Creole of Color society had already developed a complex and rigid class structure based on skin color (Willey 247). The families of the Creole of Color elite, generally those with the lightest complexions, have traditionally identified more closely with south Louisiana's white ethnic communities than with their black neighbors, despite the continuing antipathy of the white upper class. Recent studies of black Creole communities in Louisiana suggest that the group's traditional preoccupations with class status and phenotype survived intact to the present among some Creoles of Color—particularly among those individuals whose genetic makeup is at least three-fourths Caucasian. In recent decades, many of these elite Creole of Color families have maintained their traditional cultural and racial orientations, which, according to anthropologist Virginia Dominguez, remain largely based on skin color: "Colored Creoles strive for *whitening*, which amounts to a kind of process of purification. It is a process, not a fixed reality. Like other Caribbean and Afro-American groups . . . these Creoles impose a value hierarchy on the continuum of physical appearance; the whiter a person is the better his status and the blacker he is the lower his ascribed status. . . . Traditionally, these Creoles have rejected the labels *black* and *Negro* in descriptions of themselves" (1979:62–63).

Such attitudes within Louisiana's Creole of Color community over the years have resulted in an amazing number of legal challenges to legislative, administrative, and judicial attempts by the state to define race—first to deny inheritance rights to natural children, later to uphold segregation, and finally to enforce desegregation. Between 1810 and 1910 legislation and legal precedents maintained that even the most infinitesimal degree of Negro "blood" classified an individual as a "person of color." In 1910, the Louisiana Supreme Court established "1/16th traceable Negro blood" as the legal benchmark for racial classification. The court reversed itself in 1940 in the case of *Sunseri v. Cassagne* (191 La. 209), indicating that any degree of traceability was sufficient for Negro classification. This decision, which established the basis of the state's racial classification system, caused a tremendous backlash within the Creole of Color community. The Louisiana Civil Service's investigation of the state's Bureau of Vital Statistics, the office charged earlier in this century with responsibility for verifying racial designations on birth and burial certificates, had challenged literally thousands of attempts by Creoles of Color throughout Louisiana, including the prairie region, to "pass for white." Between 1960 and 1965 alone, the bureau flagged 4,700 birth certificate applications and 1,100 applications for death certificates and held them in abeyance, precipitating numerous legal challenges to the racial designations imposed upon applicants by Baton Rouge bureaucrats ostensibly on the basis of genealogical evidence of Negro "blood" (Dominguez 1979:81–83).

The amount of litigation precipitated by the Bureau of Vital Statistics system of racial flagging and the growing backlash against such segregationist labeling devices in the wake of the civil rights movement eventually attracted the attention of Louisiana's political establishment. In 1970 the state legislature modified Louisiana's legal criteria for racial identification through Act 46—"An Act to define 'colored,' 'mulatto,' 'black,' 'negro,' 'griffe,' 'Afro-American,' 'quadroon,' 'mestizo,' 'colored person' and 'person of color' when such terms are used to signify the race of a person by any public official in the state of Louisiana." This act, which remained in effect for thirteen years, arbitrarily established "1/32nd Negro blood" as the new legal benchmark for African-American racial identity.

Louisiana's racial classification criteria, in all of their myriad forms, have proven equally unpalatable to the state's Creoles of Color. Resistance to these arbitrary racial standards took various forms—legal challenges, out-migration to northern and western states, where racial classification methods were less arbitrary and less rigidly enforced, and finally to a seemingly endless series of private appeals to Louisiana's Bureau of Vital Statistics, which ultimately bore the responsibility for classifying individuals on the basis of race (Dominguez 1979:82). As late as 1976, bureau officials conceded that their staff devoted more than six thousand man-hours to challenges against racial designations imposed by the state upon Creoles of Color pursuant to the terms of Act 46 of 1970 (*New Orleans States-Item,* June 5–16, 1978).

The most notable challenge to Louisiana's racial classification system was mounted in 1982 by a prairie Creole of Color, Susie Guillory Phipps. A native of Eunice, Louisiana, then residing near Lake Charles, Phipps, who was only one-thirty-second black, maintained that she had a legal right to identify herself as white; however, the courts, citing earlier legal precedents, ruled otherwise. Phipps's challenge nevertheless proved effective in removing Louisiana's last major impediment to attempts by Creoles of Color to cross the so-called color line by forcing the state to reassess its racial classification statute.

In 1983, responding to the almost universal condemnation of the national and international press of Act 46 of 1970, which was perceived as racist (Dominguez 1986:1–3), a coalition of Louisiana legislators, led by Representative Lee Frazier of New Orleans, successfully sponsored Act 441, signed into law on July 2, 1983, which repealed the thirteen-year-old statute and effectively permitted racial self-identification (*West's Louisiana Statutes* 335). In the wake of the repeal of Act 46 of 1970, numerous young Creoles of Color—particularly children in families that moved to south Louisiana urban centers over the past two decades—began to identify themselves as white when forced by schools to indicate race (Interviews with numerous faculty members in Lafayette Parish public schools).

The long-term effect of this migratory trend across racial boundaries, of course, holds demographic implications for the Creole of Color community in the prairie parishes. Other Creoles of Color, particularly persons of a darker phenotype, have maintained the black identity forced upon the community by Louisiana's move from multiracial to biracial identification in the 1860s and solidified by the institution of segregation in the 1890s.

In the 1950s and 1960s, and especially in the 1970s and 1980s, what was once an involuntary and unwanted racial classification became a badge of honor for many young Creoles of Color involved in the civil rights movement. They not only proudly identified themselves as black but also consciously sought out the African-American aspect of their heritage. The following comments by Wilbert Guillory constitute perhaps the best distillation of these sentiments: "We lost the identity of blackness of Afro-Americans. It's through the *black Creoles* that we capture that—through unity," that is, with the African-Americans so long shunned by Creoles of Color (Foote 21).

Yet the black identification of many Creoles of Color is somewhat misleading for the consensus of the most recent published scholarship on the community indicates that most prairie Creoles of Color have consciously chosen to maintain their syncretic Afro-French cultural and mixed racial identities. One observer, writing in the late 1980s, maintains that the community's "ambivalence over solidarity with blacks versus exclusiveness of the Creoles persists in varying degrees to the present day in rural southwestern Louisiana" (Spitzer 53).

This ambivalence is seen increasingly in the popular form of self-identification within the Creole of Color community, "oriented toward pride in being both black *and* French and thus having the advantages of both strains within an individual or community. That is, black Creole people have increasingly become proud of their ancestral and cultural creolization. . . . Creoles have, in recent years, come to value the essentially bivalent properties of their ethnic identity" (Spitzer 154). Growing recognition and acceptance of the factors that have traditionally set Creoles of Color apart from their neighbors have, in recent years, sparked a resurgence of interest in traditional Creole culture, culminating in the establishment, in the late 1980s, of Creole, Inc., a major cultural organization and a vocal advocate of public recognition of Creole contributions to southwest Louisiana's development, and in the launching of *Creole Magazine,* a monthly forum for Creole social, cultural, and political issues since 1989.

The recent resurgence of southwest Louisiana's Creole of Color community reflects changes in racial attitudes in the nation as a whole, as America slowly comes to grips with the unique status and multiple racial identities of persons of mixed ancestry. With feet firmly planted in both the white and African-American worlds while straddling the issue of race, the prairie Creoles of Color have been and are likely to remain a people apart in Louisiana's complex ethnic and racial mosaic.

APPENDIX A

Civil Suits Involving Creoles of Color, Clerk of Court's Office,
St. Landry Parish Courthouse, ca. 1855–ca. 1895

compiled by Keith P. Fontenot

[NOTE: C.D.S. indicates Civil District Suit.]

Auzenne, Carlostin, administrator of Euphrasie Brunet's estate, vs. John Lyons, #8117–2, May 6, 1857. Type: Hypothecary debt. Judgment: Plaintiff.

Auzenne, Hermina, F.W.C. (a minor over 18 years of age), application for emancipation, #10088, October 4, 1866. Type: Emancipation of a minor. Judgment: Plaintiff (i.e., emancipation approved).

Bataille, Theodore C., vs. Louis Rideau, F.M.C., C.D.S. #7759, May 3, 1856. Judgment: Damages. Judgment: Dismissed.

Cambon, S., & Company, vs. Marie Louise Lemelle, wife of Joseph Delmont Donato, C.D.S. #12388, April 7, 1874. Type: Open account. Judgment: Plaintiff. [Note: The above suit refers to Marie Louise as a public merchant in the town of Opelousas. She owned property separate from her community property.]

Capitaine, Marie Ann, vs. Valmont Bloom, C.D.S. #15,361, May 21, 1894. Type: Separation. Judgment: Plaintiff.

Chenier, Joseph, vs. David Guillory, C.D.S. #10729, November 18, 1867. Type: Open account. Judgment: Dismissed.

Chenier, Laurlette, F.W.C., et al., vs. Joseph Urban, testamentary executor of the Estate of Jean-Baptiste Fossar *dit* Petalangar, C.D.S. #10016, September 21, 1866. Type: Estate. Judgment: Dismissed.

Daire, Prosper, vs. François Jean, C.D.S. #12545, May 6, 1876. Type: Promissory note. Judgment: Plaintiff.

Donato, Alicia, application for emancipation, C.D.S. #13166, June 30, 1881. Type: Emancipation of a minor. Judgment: Plaintiff.

Donato, Auguste, *fils*, F.M.C., vs. Charles Close, et al., C.D.S. #9657, February 3, 1866. Type: Executory process. Judgment: Plaintiff.

Donato, Auguste, *fils*, F.M.C., vs. Gustave E. Louaillier, et al., D.C.S. #9454, December 28, 1864. Type: Injunction. Judgment: Plaintiff.

Donato, Auguste, *fils*, vs. Julien Bordelon, C.D.S. #11093, November 6, 1869. Type: Order of seizure and sale. Judgment: Plaintiff.

Donato, George, vs. François Auguste Donato, C.D.S. #13409, December 13, 1883. Type: Partition. Judgment: For Plaintiff.

Donato, Joseph Dalmont, administrator of Adelaide C. Lesassier's estate, vs. McHenry Husband, C.D.S. #9533, October 16, 1865. Type: Injunction. Judgment: Plaintiff.

Donato, Joseph Dalmont, vs. Césare Bernascome, C.D.S. #9525, October 11, 1865. Type: Seizures and sale. Judgment: Plaintiff.

Donato, Joseph Delmont, administrator of Adelaide Céleste Lesassier's estate, vs. McHenry Husband, C.D.S. #9524, October 11, 1865. Type: Seizure and sale. Judgment: Plaintiff.

Dowling, James M. vs. Euzèbe Auzenne, #12911, October 18, 1880. Type: Open account. Judgment: Plaintiff.

Dupré, Lastie, testamentary executor of Laurent Dupré's estate, vs. Auguste Donato, *père*, et al., C.D.S. #9557, October 31, 1865. Type: Promissory note. Judgment: Dismissed.

Dupré, Lastie, testamentary executor of Laurent Dupré's estate, vs. Cornelius Donato, et al., C.D.S. #9717, February 27, 1866. Type: Promissory note. Judgment: Plaintiff.

Dupré, Lastie, testamentary executor of Laurent Dupré's estate, vs. Cornelius Donato, et al., C.D.S. #9718, February 27, 1866. Type: Promissory note. Judgment: Dismissed.

Dupré, Lastie, testamentary executor of Laurent Dupré's estate, vs. Cornelius Donato, et al., C.D.S. #10938, June 1, 1868. Type: Injunction. Judgment: Plaintiff.

Dupré, Lastie, testamentary executor of Laurent Dupré's estate, vs. Widow of Sabin Donato, F.W.C., Zenon Rideau, and Louis Rideau, C.D.S. #9711, February 26, 1866. Type: Promissory note. Judgment: Plaintiff.

Dupré, Lastie, testamentary executor of the estate of Laurent Dupré, vs. Cornelius Donato, et al., C.D.S. #9645, January 29, 1866. Type: Promissory note. Judgment: Plaintiff.

Dupré, Lucius J., administrator of Cyprien Dupré's estate, vs. Théotiste Esprit, et al., C.D.S. #10893, April 21, 1868. Type: Promissory note. Judgment: Plaintiff.

Dupré, Lucius J., administrator of the estate of Cyprien Dupré, vs. Norbert Malveaux, F.M.C., et al., C.D.S. #9861, April 28, 1866. Type: Promissory note. Judgment: Plaintiff.

Durand, Jean-Marie, vs. George Simien, F.M.C., C.D.S. #9352, March 21, 1862. Type: Open account, appeal from justice of the peace court. Judgment: Plaintiff, at justice of the peace court; no judgment located for district court suit.

Esprit, Bonnet, vs. François Thierry, C.D.S. #5199, April 14, 1849. Type: Damages. Judgment: Defendant.

First National Bank of Opelousas vs. Adelaide Frilot, et al., C.D.S. #15247, June 28, 1895. Type: Promissory note. Judgment: Dismissed.

Fontenot, Augustin B., F.M.C., vs. Olivrel B. Fontenot, F.M.C., C.D.S.: 9672, February 10, 1866. Type: Tutorship. Judgment: Dismissed. [Note: The term "F.M.C." is not listed in the lawsuit, but rather in a *sale and agreement* in C.O.B. U-1, p. 361, #7545, December 14, 1866.]

Fontenot, Théophile S., et al., vs. Louis Cadé Malveaux, C.D.S. #14697, September 17, 1890. Type: Provisional land seizure. Judgment: Dismissed. [Note: A land dispute in the Plaisance area.]

Frilot, Denis, application for emancipation, C.D.S. #14152, October 15, 1886. Type: Emancipation of a minor. Judgment: Approved.

Frilot, Jos. Euzèbe, application for emancipation, C.D.S. #14151, October 15, 1886. Type: Emancipation of a minor. Judgment: Approved.

Froidevaux, Edouard, vs. Rose Thierry, F.W.C., C.D.S. #8850, October 3, 1859. Type: Open account. Judgment: Dismissed.

Gallot, Julien, F.M.C., vs. Victoire Guillory, F.W.C., his wife, C.D.S. #8950, May 3, 1860. Type: Custody. Judgment: Plaintiff. [Note: The couple's children included: Catherine, Victoire, Julien, Delogue, Lenore, Herminia, Evariste and Victor Gallot.]

Gallot, Julien, F.M.C., vs. Victoire Guillory, his wife, C.D.S. #9882, May 28, 1866. Type: Divorce. Judgment: Plaintiff.

Garland, Henry L., vs. Villeneuve Rideau, et al., C.D.S. #16021, February 18, 1897. Type: Promissory notes, seizure. Judgment: Plaintiff.

Giguel and Jamieson vs. Rose Thierry, F.W.C., C.D.S. #10018, September 21, 1866. Type: Promissory note. Judgment: Plaintiff.

Guillory, Lastie, vs. Alexandre Papillion, *fils*, C.D.S. #13881, February 23, 1885. Type: Slander. Judgment: Jury rendered verdict for defendant and suit dismissed at plaintiff's cost.

Guillory, Marcelite, F.W.C., vs. Jean-Baptiste Durisseau, administrator of Auguste Durouseau's estate, C.D.S. #10284, October 30, 1866. Type: Labor lien. Judgment: Dismissed.

Guillory, Martin, vs. Jeanne Lemelle, his wife, C.D.S. #12298, January 15, 1873. Type: Divorce. Judgment: Plaintiff.

Harmon, Solomon B., vs. Firman Lemelle, C.D.S. #10150, October 13, 1866. Type: Damages. Judgment: Not located.

Henry, Arsène, vs. Josette Chrétien, F.W.C., C.D.S. #10664, November 21, 1867. Type: Promissory note. Judgment: Plaintiff.

Isaac, Solomon, vs. Jean-Baptiste Rideau, C.D.S. #14231, May 7, 1887. Type: Promissory note. Judgment: Plaintiff.

Jean, Arthur, husband, vs. Charlotte Mayfield, wife, C.D.S. #14557, October 29, 1889. Type: Divorce. Judgment: Plaintiff.

Jean, François, F.M.C., vs. Joseph Hollier, administrator of Julien C. Gonor's estate, C.D.S. #7771, May 7, 1856. Type: Open account. Judgment: Plaintiff.

Jean, François, F.M.C., vs. Kinchen W. McKinney, C.D.S. #10774, Dec. 27, 1867. Type: Promissory note. Judgment: Not indicated.

Jean, François, vs. C. C. Duson, sheriff, C.D.S. #12524, February 4, 1876. Type: Injunction. Judgment: Plaintiff.

Jean, Jean François, vs. Pauline Jean, tutrix ad hoc, #13253, February 25, 1882. Type: Executory. Judgment: Plaintiff.

Jones, Ellebe, vs. Felicité Rideau, #15695, October 8, 1895. Type: Separation and custody. Judgment: Plaintiff: Defendant ordered to return to matrimonial domicile. [Note: Felicité Rideau was the daughter of Villeneuve Rideau. Four children: Peltore P., Wayhamel P., Elverda, and Jo Nathan Jones. Married: December 13, 1887.]

Landreneau, Joseph J., vs. Treville Rideau, C.D.S. #15282, November 2, 1893. Type: Seizure. Judgment: Plaintiff.

Lartigue, Julien, vs. Angeline Lartigue, F.P.C., C.D.S. #9364, April 23, 1862. Type: Interdiction. Judgment: Not located.

Ledé, Augustin, F.M.C., vs. Julien Guillory, F.M.C., C.D.S. #8868, October 18, 1859. Type: Appeal. Judgment: Plaintiff, in Justice of the Peace Court. [Note: This is an appeal from Joseph Chenier, Justice of the Peace, Eighth Ward, St. Landry Parish. Justice of the Peace Chenier ruled for the plaintiff. No district court judgment.]

Lehman, Abraham & Co., vs. Euphémie A. Thierry, et al., C.D.S. #13845, December 27, 1884. Judgment: Seizure. Judgment: Dismissed. [Note: Euphémie Thierry was the wife of Jean Baptiste Rideau, but separated in property. Moreover, reference is made to the Jean Baptiste Rideau plantation located at Plaisance, Saint Landry Parish. The suit related to an agricultural lease.]

Lehman, Abraham, & Co., vs. Jean-Baptiste Rideau, C.D.S. #13475, February 10, 1883. Type: Breach of contract. Judgment: Not located.

Lemelle, Firmin, F.M.C., of Calcasieu Parish, tutor of Josephine U. Magunin, F.W.C., final accounting of, C.D.S. #8682, April 11, 1859. Type: Tutorship. Judgment: Homologated final account.

Lemelle, Firmin, F.M.C., vs. François Robin, et al., tutors of the Heirs of Marie Louise Lemelle, F.W.C., and the Heirs of Félicité Coffigne, F.W.C., C.D.S. #5738, October 27, 1851. Type: Tutorship, etc. Judgment: Plaintiff.

Lemelle, François, F.M.C., administrator of the Estate of Louise Frilot, his wife, vs. Benjamin Dejean, C.D.S. #10643, November 11, 1867. Type: Hypothecary debt. Judgment: Dismissed.

Lemelle, Ludger, et al., vs. François Lemelle, administrator, C.D.S. #10813, January 25, 1868. Type: Tutorship. Judgment: Plaintiff.

Lemelle, Ludger, et al., vs. François Lemelle, C.D.S. #12843, July 10, 1880. Type: Estate. Judgment: Plaintiff.

Lemelle, Ludger, et al., vs. James M. Thompson and James M. Thompson vs. Ludger Lemelle, C.D.S. #12745–12746. Type: Executory. Judgment: Plaintiff.

Lemelle, Marie Louise, vs. Joseph Delmont Donato, her husband, C.D.S.: #11013, January 7, 1869. Type: Paraphernal. Judgment: Plaintiff.

Lemelle, Martin, vs. Jeanne Lemelle, C.D.S. #12298, January 15, 1873. Type: Divorce. Judgment: Plaintiff.

Lemelle, Virginia, F.W.C., wife of Philippe Esterling, vs. Auguste Donato, F.M.C., tutor, of the Heirs of Alfred Lemelle, F.M.C., C.D.S. #7574, October 18, 1855. Type: Judicial partition. Judgment: Plaintiff.

Lewis, Thomas H., et al., vs. Celesie Malveaux, F.W.C., et al., C.D.S. #8467, May 7, 1858. Type: Promissory note. Judgment: Plaintiff.

Lewis, William B., et ux., vs. Antoine St. André, F.M.C., C.D.S. #10775, December 28, 1867. Type: Provisional seizure. Judgment: Plaintiff.

Malveau, Sebastien, F.M.C., vs. Marianne Duchesne, his wife, F.W.C., C.D.S. #9408, February 2, 1863. Type: Separation. Judgment: Dismissed.

Malveau, Sebastien, vs. Marianne Duchesne, his wife, C.D.S. #11029, January 11, 1869. Type: Divorce. Judgment: Plaintiff. [Note: The defendant lived in concubinage with Jean-Baptiste Rideau.]

Masse, Caroline, F.W.C., vs. Eleonor Young, F.W.C., C.D.S. #7714, Apr. 3, 1856. Type: Seizure and sale. Judgment: No judgment indicated.

Meuillon, Antoine Alphonse, F.M.C., application for motion, C.D.S. #9997, September 13, 1866. Type: Motion. Judgment: Plaintiff.

Meyers, J., & Co., vs. Jean Baptiste Rideau, C.D.S. #13480, February 28, 1883. Type: Open account. Judgment: Dismissed.

Miller & Forestier vs. Severine Ramard, F.W.C., C.D.S. #8537, September 6, 1858. Type: Promissory note. Judgment: Dismissed.

Mornhinveg, Christian, Sr., vs. Joseph Lemelle alias Collins, C.D.S. #13152, November 7, 1881. Type: Lien. Judgment: Dismissed.

Mornhinveg, Christian, Sr., vs. Joseph Lemelle alias Collins, C.D.S. #13157, November 19, 1881. Type: Sequestration. Judgment: Plaintiff.

Mouton, Adolphe Alex, vs. Jean Baptiste Rideau, C.D.S. #13257, March 10, 1882. Type: Open account. Judgment: Not located.

Parker, James H., vs. Treville Rideau, C.D.S. #15376, May 10, 1894. Type: Promissory note. Judgment: Plaintiff.

Patin, Emelia vs. Josette Chrétien, F.W.C., C.D.S. #8117–1, May 5, 1857. Type: Promissory note. Judgment: Plaintiff.

Perissin, Jean B., vs. Alexandre Auzenne, F.M.C., #8564, September 30, 1858. Type: Promissory note. Judgment: Suit dismissed at plaintiff's cost.

Perrodin, Auguste, liquidator of the firm of J. & A. Perrodin, vs. Rudolph Malveaux, et al., C.D.S. #13503, March 20, 1883. Type: Promissory note. Judgment: Plaintiff.

Perrodin, Auguste, liquidator of A. & J. Perrodin, vs. Adolphe Malveau, C.D.S. #14347, March 7, 1888. Type: Promissory note. Judgment: Plaintiff.

Perrodin, Auguste, liquidator of the firm of J. & A. Perrodin, vs. Adolphe Malveaux, C.D.S. #13501, March 20, 1883. Type: Hypothecary debt. Judgment: Plaintiff.

Phelps, Noah H., vs. Severine Ramard, F.W.C., C.D.S. #9145, March 5, 1861. Type: Promissory note. Judgment: Dismissed.

Pigeon, Frédéric, et al., vs. Rose Thierry, C.D.S. #7897, September 23, 1856. Type: Appeal from justice of the peace court. Judgment: Dismissed.

Prudhomme, Dorsin, vs. Julien Thierry, C.D.S. #13633, November 2, 1883. Type: Slander. Judgment: Not located.

Quatreveaux, Narcisse, vs. Joseph Gradenigo, F.M.C., administrator of James Edmonds' estate, C.D.S. #7769, May 6, 1856. Type: Judicial partition. Judgment: Plaintiff.

Rideau, Preval, agent and attorney in fact for Lucy Lafleur, and Hyacinthe Lafleur vs. Jean-Baptiste Rideau, C.D.S. #13596, September 17, 1883. Type: Promissory note. Judgment: Plaintiff.

Rideau, Zenon, F.M.C., vs. District Attorney, C.D.S. #7646, March 1, 1856. Type: Slave emancipation. Judgment: Plaintiff by default.

Rideau, Zenon, vs. Adeline Durio, C.D.S. #13347, September 6, 1882. Type: Land title. Judgment: Dismissed. [Note: Zenon Rideau was a resident St. Martin Parish. The land in litigation was located in St. Martin Parish.]

Rideau, Zenon, vs. Sheriff C. C. Duson, et al., C.D.S. #13142, October 20, 1881. Type: Injunction. Judgment: Plaintiff.

Roos, David, vs. Elizée Lemelle, C.D.S. #14532, September 6, 1889. Type: Damages. Judgment: Plaintiff.

Smith, J. S., vs. Sosthène Malveau, F.M.C., C.D.S. #10665, November 21, 1867. Type: Promissory note. Judgment: Plaintiff.

Stewart, Stephen, vs. Jean François Jean, administrator of François Jean's estate, C.D.S. #13129, September 23, 1881. Type: Damages. Judgment: Dismissed.

Thieri, Rose, F.W.C., vs. Euphoisine Deshautels, wife of Raymond Deshautels, C.D.S. #10923, May 20, 1868. Type: Open account. Judgment: Not located.

Thierry, Bernard, vs. A. Pierrel, C.D.S. #8927, April 7, 1860. Type: Promissory note. Judgment: Not located. [Note: Bernard Thierry resided in France.]

Thierry, Euphémie Alexandre, vs. Jean Baptiste Rideau, her husband, C.D.S. #13613, September 27, 1883. Type: Paraphernal. Judgment: Plaintiff.

Wilkins, Robert S., vs. Irene Thierry, C.D.S. #13192, January 2, 1882. Type: Promissory note. Judgment: Plaintiff.

Transactions Involving Creoles of Color Conveyance Books, Clerk of Court's Office, St. Landry Parish Courthouse

Compiled by Claude Oubre

Listed herein are selected conveyances involving Creoles of Color from the following nine families: Auzenne, Aubespin, Donato (Donatto, Donate), Frilot, Lemelle, Malveau, Meuillon, Rideau, and Semien (Simien). These conveyances were found in the records of the Clerk of Court, St. Landry Parish, and cover the years 1860 to 1886. The majority of the conveyances selected fell during the crucial years of Reconstruction when free people of color were forced to deal with the changes resulting from the end of slavery. The Guillory family is conspicuous by its absence. Because of the difficulty involved in determining the race of the parties in a conveyance as a result of the abundance of both white and black Guillorys, the authors chose to exclude this family rather than risk the inclusion of questionable data. Other Creole of Color families such as Birotte, Boutté, Durousseau, Fuselier, Gaubert, Godeau, Ledé or Ledet, Malveau, Paillet, and Papillon are included only if the spouse is a member of one of the above nine families.

Auzenne, Aubespin, and wife to Estelle Garrigues, widow of Louis Vanhille, Original act #11517, Book Y-1, p. 585. On September 18, 1871, Auzenne sold Garrigues 41.74 arpents of land one mile south of the town of Washington for the price of $1,000.

Auzenne, Cadmus, to Francis Hollier, sheriff's sale, Book X-1, p. 370. On March 5, 1870, the sheriff seized and sold at public auction three tracts of land belonging to Cadmus Auzenne; one was described as a 16.25-arpent tract, one was a 20.5-arpent tract, and the third was described as woodland in Prairie Basse. Hollier held a mortgage and bid the value of his mortgage.

Auzenne, Carlostin, estate of, to Cadmus Auzenne and Estelle Auzenne, Public Auction, located between original acts 7475 and 7477, Book U-1, p. 327. On November 14, 1866 the estate sold a half square of lot #37 in the town of Washington to Cadmus and Estelle, who was assisted by her husband Agenor Giron, for the price of $2,500.

Auzenne, Carlostin, estate of, to Laurette Guidry, F.W.C., wife of Theodore

Chenier, F.M.C., Public Auction, Book U-1, p. 327. On November 14, Laurette Guidry entered the high bid of $1,200 for half lot #55 in town of Washington, Louisiana.

Auzenne, Philogene, and his wife, Clementine Meuillon, to Azolin Savoie, original act #9592, Book X-1, p. 429. On April 8, 1870, Auzenne sold Savoie 121.4 acres of land in Prairie Basse of Grand Coteau along Bayou Bourbeau, identified as being lots 4, 5, and 6 of section 6 of Township 8 South, Range 4 East for the price of $200.

Bernascome, César, to Joseph Delmont Donato, Sheriff sale, Book X-1, p. 227. In 1860, Donato loaned Bernascome $1300 to buy lots in Opelousas. Since no payment had ever been made and Donato had filed suit in St. Landry Parish District Court, the parties agreed to exchange the note for the lots.

Close, Jean Pierre, Charles Close Administrator, to Gustave Donato, Sheriff Sale, Book U-1, p. 103. On April 12, 1866, Gustave Donato entered the high bid on a tract of land containing six by sixty-five arpents fronting on Bayou Teche and being part of the old *vacherie* tract. The sale resulted from St. Landry District Court Suit #9657, Auguste Donato, *fils,* v. Charles Close, administrator.

Debaillon, Alexandrine Ann Louaillier, to Bello Auguste Donato, original act # 7620, Book U-1, p. 399. On January 17, 1867, Mrs. Debaillon sold Donato a twenty-four-arpent tract of land located two miles south of Opelousas for the price of $490.60.

Debaillon, Alexandrine Ann Louallier, widow of Evariste Debaillon, to Emelie Fuselier, wife of Philip Frilot, original act #8406, Book V-1, p. 99. On June 20, 1868, Mrs. Debaillon sold Emelie a tract of land with two arpents front on the public road from Opelousas to Bayou Teche for the price of $80 in gold. This was land which Mrs. Debaillon had inherited from her mother, Marie Cain. [See companion sale to Emelie's sister Rose Aimée which follows.]

Debaillon, Alexandrine Ann Louallier, widow of Evariste Debaillon, to Rose Aimée Fuselier. Original act #8405, Book v-1, p. 99. On June 20, 1868, Mrs. Debaillon sold Rose Fuselier a four-arpent tract described as two arpents front by two arpents depth on the road from Opelousas to Bayou Teche.

Donato, Ann, wife of Edouard Fuselier [lives in the quartier Plaisance], to Hilaire Chenier, original act #6992, Book U-1, p. 70. On March 5, 1866, Mrs Fuselier sold Chenier a tract of land north and near the city of Opelousas having two arpents front by six arpents depth. The land was originally purchased from feu Félicité Paillet, wife of Valmont Gradenigo from the succession of Antoine Paillet.

Donato, Auguste, *fils* [formerly a resident of New Orleans, now a resident of

St. Landry], to Joseph Leonard Estorge, original act #11011, book Y-1, p. 248.
On February 8, 1871, Auguste Donato sold Joseph Estorge a tract of land
near Barre's Landing known as the old *vacherie* containing six arpents front
on Bayou Teche by sixty-five arpents deep. Donato had purchased the land
at a sheriff sale in execution of a judgment against Julien Bordelon in May
1870. After reacquiring the land at the sheriff's sale, Donato leased the plantation to Bordelon on May 10, 1870. See Miscellaneous Book 4, p. 375.
[Here we have an interesting turnaround. Bordelon, who was white, initially purchased the land from the Donatos. During Reconstruction he lost
possession of the land and became the tenant of Auguste Donato, a Creole
of Color. Apparently the lease between Donato and Bordelon was only for
the crop year because early the following year, Donato sold to Estorge, another white person.]

Donato, Auguste, to Marie Louise Lemelle, wife of Joseph Delmont Donato,
Original act #11571, Book Z-1, p. 1. On November 8, 1871, Donato sold
Marie Louise Lemelle Donato a town lot in Opelousas described as Lot #2
on North Street with dimensions of 100.5 × 169.5 feet, for a price of $2000.
[Marie Louise bought this as her own separate property; she had secured a
court order allowing her to control her separate property.]

Donato, Auguste, *père*, estate of, public auction, Book C-2, pp. 588–95. On
December 20, 1875, the administrators sold the real property belonging to
the estate of Auguste Donato, *père*, located on the road to Washington and
Flat Town. The property was divided into twenty-four tracts of farmland
and eighteen tracts of woodland. Seven individuals purchased all the tracts
for a total of $11,426.89. The purchasers were identified as Cléophas Co-
meau, Mrs. Edmund (Amynthe) Dupré, Mrs. Céleste Garland, J. K. San-
doz, John N. Ogden, Thomas C. Anderson, and Louis Prudhomme.

Donato, Clarissa, estate of, to Gustave Donato, public auction, Book A-2
p. 591. On November 26, 1873, Gustave Donato entered the high bid of
$1,500 for a lot and a half lot in the town of Opelousas, identified as lots #9
and the north half of #10 on North Street and Main Street.

Donato, Cornelius, to Hylaire Tate, Junior, original act #4959, Book T-1, p. 72.
On January 16, 1861, Donato sold Tate a Negro slave named Joseph, eighteen years of age, for the price of $1,200.

Donato, Elizabeth, estate of, to Antoine Alphonse Meuillon, Anne Elizabeth
Meuillon, wife of Simon Birotte, Marianne Teramine Meuillon, wife of
Pierre E. Frilot, Marie Clementine Meuillon, wife of Jacques Auzenne, Lu-
cien Terance Meuillon, Leocadie Meuillon, wife of Jules Pierre Frilot, Jean
Baptiste Meuillon, and Armand Meuillon. Act of Partition, original act
#11214, Book Y-1, p. 384. On April 17, 1871, the eight heirs divided the land
of the estate in Prairie Laurent on Bayou Teche. Each received one-eighth of

the total frontage on the bayou. [See also Antoine D. Meuillon to Heirs of Elizabeth Donato, below, original act #7003.]

Donato, Gustave, and his wife, Marie Anne Lassassier, to Julien Bordelon [lives near Rider Bridge], original act # 7054, Book U-1, p. 107. On April 15, 1866, Donato sold to Bordelon a piece of property near Barre's landing on Bayou Teche described as the old *vacherie* containing six arpents front by sixty-five arpents depth. The land had been acquired in the case of Auguste Donato, *fils*, in his suit against Charles Close. There is a note in the margin of the conveyance dated August 27, 1867, indicating that $500 was paid to Auguste Donato, *fils*, by A. B. Martel.

Donato, Julie, wife of Joseph Esprit, with his permission, to Eugene David, original act # 6234, Book T-1, p. 562. On June 5, 1863, Donato sold David a mulatto woman slave named Eustine, seventeen years of age, for the price of $1,500.

Donato, Julie, estate of, to Eugenie Donato, widow of Leon Manse, public auction by Emile Donato, administrator, Book C-2, page 795. On March 14, 1876, Eugenie Donato entered the high bid of $1,000 for two lots of ground and buildings in the town of Opelousas on the road to Washington.

Donato, Mrs. Sabin, F.W.C. [Magdeleine Robin, widow] to François Dupré, original act # 6406, Book T-1, p. 610. On December 8, 1863, Mrs. Donato sold François Dupré a mulatto slave named Etienne, fourteen years of age, for the price of $1,675.

Emonet, Michael, to Victor Auzenne, original act #9864, Book Y-1 p. 46. On October 13, 1870, Emonet sold Victor Auzenne a tract of land having three arpents front by six arpents depth in Prairie Gros Chevreuil for the price of $300.

Follain, Gerand, through his agent Cornelius Donato [Follain, at the time of the conveyance was a resident of Matamoras, Mexico; Cornelius was his brother-in-law], to Jean-Baptiste Lavergne, F.M.C., original act # 7, Book U-1, p. 340. On November 29, 1866, Donato sold to Lavergne an eighty-three-arpent tract of land located in the Mallet Woods. [The ratification by Gerand Follain of this conveyance is in Book U-1, p. 547.]

Frilot, Mrs. Hilaire (Leontine Lemelle), with his permission, to Charles E. Lemelle, original act #8388, Book V-1, p. 94. On June 6, 1868, Mrs. Frilot sold Charles Lemelle a town lot in Opelousas. This was the lot she had purchased previously at a sheriff's sale on December 11, 1865, in the case of Joseph D. Donato, administrator, for the succession of Adelaide C. Lesassier, against McHenry Husband.

Frilot, Louis, and wife, Cecile Lemelle, to Joseph Frilot, original act # 7683, Book U-1, p. 431. On February 7, 1867, Louis Frilot sold Joseph Frilot a tract of land in Prairie Plaisance containing three arpents front by twenty arpents deep for the price of $700. This was the tract Louis had purchased from Joseph Chauvin on March 27, 1860, recorded in book L-1, p. 444.

Frilot, Louis Hilaire, and his wife, Leontine Lemelle, to Ann Paillet, widow of Louis Frilot, previously widow of Martin Donato, original act # 8939, Book V-1, p. 467. On August 10, 1869, Louis H. Frilot sold Ann Paillet an undivided one-half portion of a lot in Opelousas with an eighty-foot front. This was the same land that Ann Paillet had sold to him on December 29, 1866, recorded in Book U-1, p. 376 (see next entry).

Frilot, Veuve Louis [Anne Paillet Donato Frilot] to Hilaire Louis Frilot, original act # 7581, Book U-1, p. 376. On December 29, 1866, Mrs. Frilot sold a lot of land in Opelousas having eighty-foot front on Union Street for the price of $200. This was land she purchased from the Louallier Succession.

Frilot, Veuve Louis (Marie Cecile Lemelle, as tutor of her minor children), to Jean Baptiste Rideau, original act #11186, Book Y-1, p. 368. On April 11, 1871, Veuve Louis Frilot sold Jean Baptiste Rideau a tract of land in Prairie Plaisance described as being 196 feet by 150 feet for the price of $800. The land is further described as having been land which the deceased had purchased from Jean Baptiste Rideau on March 30, 1870, and recorded in Book X-1, p. 410. [Because of the date of purchase and the different name for the veuve evidently this is Louis Frilot, Junior's widow.]

Frilot, Pierre Jules, and his wife, Leocadie Meuillon, to Antoine Pain, original act # 7396, Book U-1, p. 284. On October 17, 1866, Frilot sold Pain his *habitation* on the left bank of Bayou Teche containing 67.75 arpents for the price of $850. Pain paid $800 in gold and $50 in U.S. bills. This was land which Frilot had purchased from the succession of Antoine Mayer, April 8, 1859.

Garland, Céleste Lastrapes, to Ozenne Aubespin, F.M.C., original act # 7202, Book U-1, p. 173. On July 7, 1866, Mrs. Garland sold Aubespin a 41.74-arpent tract located one mile south of Washington, Louisiana, for the price of $417.

Godeau, Felicien, F.M.C. to Jules Godeau, F.M.C., husband of Eugenie Rideau, original act # 7014, Book U-1, p. 80. On March 24, 1866, Felicien sold Jules a ninety-acre tract of land at Tauper Flat adjoining the land of Zenon Rideau.

Husband, McHenry, to Leontine Lemelle, wife of Hilaire Frilot, original act # 6804, Book T-1, p. 702. On December 4, 1865, at a sheriff's sale, Mrs. Frilot entered the high bid of $1,300 on property to which she held a mortgage. [See Leontine Lemelle to don Louis Lemelle below.]

Hollier, Mrs. Luke [Ephrasie Roy], to Eugenie Donato, wife of Leon Manse, F.M.C., original act # 6772, Book T-1, p. 691. On November 18, 1865, Mrs.

Appendix B

139

Hollier sold Eugenie Donato Manse a town lot in Opelousas with a 110-foot front on Landry Street, immediately to the west of Tesson Coulee. [This is the area currently known as the Bottom.]

Jeannot, Pierre, to Julien J. Rideau, original act # 7616 Book U-1, p. 397. On January 16, 1867, Jeannot sold Rideau a parcel of land in Prairie Plaisance containing two superficial arpents for the price of $75.

King, Isaiah and William, to Zenon Rideau, original act # 5252, Book T-1, p. 218. On April 29, 1861, the Kings sold Rideau 40.22 acres in section 12 of Township 4 South, Range 5 East for $10 per acre or a total of $402.20. This is in the vicinity of Palmetto.

Lastrapes, Alfred, to Philogene Auzenne and Azolin Savoie, original act #7995, Book U-1, p. 603. On August 17, 1867, Lastrapes sold Auzenne and Savoie a 121.4-acre tract of land near Bayou Bourbeau in Prairie Basse of Grand Coteau for a price of $660. They paid $600 cash and for the remaining $60 they promised to provide Lastrapes with one thousand pieu of nine feet. The property is further described as lots 2, 3, 4, and 5 of Section 6, Township 8 South, Range 4 East.

Lastrapes, Céleste (widow of Rice Garland), to Marie Louise Lemelle, wife of Joseph D. Donato, original act #12399, Book Z-1, p. 598. On December 5, 1872, Mrs Lastrapes sold Mrs Donato a tract of land containing 62.7 acres for the price of $1,522.46. Mrs. Donato purchased this as her separate property. She had a court order separating her property from that of her husband.

Lawrence, Henry, to François Semien, land retrocession, Book U-1, p. 181. On July 27, 1866, Lawrence returned to Semien a tract of land in Bayou Mallet woods, partly woodland and partly prairie, containing five arpents front on Bayou Mallet by forty arpents deep. This is land Semien had sold to Lawrence on May 28, 1860.

Lavigne, Adele Narcisse, widow of Louis Rideau to Jean Baptiste Rideau, *fils*, represented by his father, Jean Baptiste Rideau, original act #11853, Book Z-1, p. 229. On March 14, 1872, Adele L. Rideau sold Jean Baptiste Rideau, *fils*, two tracts of land in Prairie Plaisance. The first tract contained four arpents front by twenty-two arpents deep together with one-half of all buildings and improvements. The second tract contained ten arpents front with a depth of eight arpents. The sale price was $600 for both tracts.

LeJeune, Etienne, *fils*, to François Simien, original act #12300, Book Z-1, p. 547. On November 12, 1872, LeJeune sold Simien a forty-acre tract in Bois Mallet.

Lemelle, Leontine, to Don Louis Lemelle, original act #6803, Book T-1, p. 702. On December 5, 1865, Leontine Lemelle sold Don Louis Lemelle a town lot for $620. This was a lot she had purchased at a sheriff's sale in the case of Joseph Donato v. McHenry Husband.

Lemelle, Marie Louise, and Joseph D. Donato, to Leontine Lemelle, wife of Hilaire Frilot, original act # 8014, Book U-1, p. 610. On September 2, 1867, Marie Louise and Joseph Donato sold Leontine Lemelle two town lots described as lots # 7 and #10 of the partition of Mrs. Mace on Court and Market streets for the price of $500. This was land Mrs. Donato had purchased in 1859 from Thérèse Castille, veuve de Pierre Labyche.

Lemelle, Marie Louise, wife of Joseph D. Donato to Washington Gails, original act #11611, Book Z-1, p. 45. On November 29, 1871, Marie Louise Donato sold Washington Gails Lot #19 in the Church addition of Opelousas for the price of $150. She did not need her husband's permission to sell because she was "separated in property from her said husband by judgment of District Court."

Lemelle, Martin, to David Saizon, original act #5481, Book T-1 p. 307. On October 29, 1861, Lemelle sold Saizon a five-arpent front tract of land on the corner of the road to Auzenne's Bridge and the road to Prairie Laurent for the price of $200. This was land he had acquired in the partition between Felix Auzenne, Martin Lemelle, and Alexander Auzenne on September 28, 1853.

Lemelle, Martin, to Conrad Speyrer, original act #5482, Book T-1, p. 308. On October 29, 1861, Martin Lemelle sold Conrad Speyrer a two-arpent front by fifty-arpent deep tract of land on the corner of the road from Opelousas to Prairie Laurent and the road to Grand Coteau for the price of $200.

Lemon, Pierre, *fils,* to Ludger Birotte and Simeon Birotte, husband of Anne Elizabeth Meuillon, original act #12062, Book Z-1, p. 371. On July 1, 1872, Pierre Lemon, *fils,* sold to the Birotte brothers his plantation in Prairie Laurent. The property sold was described as having four arpents front by eighty arpents depth, together with all buildings, ten head of gentle horned cattle (brand CHL), three mules (one American and two creole), two pairs of oxen, and four horses with all implements for the price of $2,500.

Meuillon, Antoine D., to the heirs of his deceased spouse, Elizabeth Donato, original act # 7003, Book U-1, pp. 73–75. The heirs are identified as Antoine Alphonse Meuillon, Anne Elizabeth Meuillon, wife of Simeon Birotte, Marianne Teramine, wife of Pierre E. Frilot, Marie Clementine Meuillon, wife of Jacques Auzenne, Lucien Terance Meuillon, Leocadie Meuillon, wife of Jules Pierre Frilot, Jean Baptiste Meuillon, and Armand Meuillon. On March 20, 1866, Antoine D. Meuillon acknowledged that he was indebted to his children to the amount of $13,045.85, community and separate property. The amounts are identified as follows:

$8,516.05 from her grandfather, Martin Donato
$1,529.80 from her deceased brother Lucien Donato
$5,529.80 the residue of one-half the community property.

Antoine Meuillon transferred to his children the following described property: The home place in Prairie Laurent on the right bank of Bayou Teche having a front of ten arpents by a depth of fifty-four arpents. He valued this property at $8,640

Six creole horses and one creole mule—	$250
Two pair of work oxen	— $50
Thirty head of horned cattle	— $270
Farming utensils	— $50
Household furniture	— $200
Total	$9,460.00

Meuillon acknowledged that he still owed his heirs $3,585.85.

Meuillon, Marie, wife of Alphonse Meuillon, and Marie Josephine Lasassier, act of partition, original act #19697, Book I-2, p 540. On May 2, 1881, Marie Meuillon and Marie Lasassier divided a tract of land described as being located on the right bank of Bayou Teche in Prairie Laurent having a five-arpent front by a depth of fifty-four arpents on four of said arpents and fifty arpents depth on the remaining arpent. Marie Meuillon took the upper half—two and one-half arpents front by fifty and fifty-four depth. Marie Josephine Lasassier took the lower half—two and one-half arpents front by fifty-four arpents depth. This was property they owned jointly through their heirship of the estates of François Lemelle and François Meuillon. François Meuillon had acquired them through two acts of partition of the estate of his parents, Baptiste Meuillon and Céleste Donato, on January 17, 1842, and on May 13, 1844. The fencing on the plantation belonged to Alphonse Meuillon and was reserved by him.

Meuillon, Suzanne Belazaire, to Auguste Donato, *fils,* original act # 5142, Book T-1, p. 169. On March 22, 1861, Suzanne Meuillon gave her nephew Auguste the following slaves: Raymond, Negro, twenty years; Cecile, Negresse, sixteen years; and her child, Bertrand, five months.

Meuillon, Suzanne Belazaire, to Gustave Donato, original act #5143, Book T-1, p. 169. On March 22, 1861, Suzanne Meuillon gave her nephew Gustave the following slaves: Simon, Negro, twenty-two years, and Annette, Negresse, fourteen years.

Meuillon, Suzanne Belazaire, estate of, to Alphonse Meuillon and Urbin Alcindor, Book Z-1, pp. 241–42. On March 6, 1872, the real property of Suzanne Belazaire Meuillon was sold at public auction. The property, a two-

hundred-arpent tract of land on Bayou Teche in Prairie Laurent near Auzenne's bridge, was divided into four-fifty-arpent lots, each with bayou
frontage of one and one-fourth arpent. Alphonse Meuillon entered the high
bid of $187 on the first tract and $185 on the second tract. Urbin Alcindor
entered the high bid of $200 on the third tract and $400 on the fourth
tract. All of the personal property of the estate was sold to numerous purchasers at public auction. The total realized from the auction of all property
belonging to the estate was $1,906.

Mire, Joseph, to Frances William, F.W.C., minor daughter of Patsy Brown,
F.W.C., wife of Don Louis Lemelle, F.M.C., original act # 7745, Book V-1,
p. 472. On February 25, 1867, Mire sold William a certain parcel of land
situated partly in the town of Opelousas, being six arpents, for the price of
$500. The adjacent landowners were North, Joseph Waillor, Michael Bor-
delon, and Gilbert Amy, East, Thomas C. Anderson, South, Joseph Waillor,
and West Melinda H. Tompson. [This would place the land in the vicinity
of Northeast Elementary and the Indian Hills Subdivision in present-day
Opelousas.] The document also contains the following note: "The said
amount [$500] is a donation made by the said mother, Pasty Brown, to her
daughter before her marriage with her said husband. And the said Pasty
Brown promises and binds herself to cause the said Frances William to ratify
the present sale when she arrives at the age of majority, either by marriage
or otherwise."

Moss, George, and wife, Nancy, to Zenon Rideau, original act # 7988, Book
U-1, p. 600. On July 32, 1867, Moss sold Rideau his plantation and all
buildings on Bayou Petite Prairie containing 160.97 acres in Sections 8 and
9, Township 4 South, Range 5 East for the price of $3,000. Terms of the
sale were $250 cash to vendor, $1,131.90 cash to judgment against Moss by
Isaac Levy and Brothers. The balance was payable to Moss secured by two
promissory notes.

Nezat, Lastie, to Cadmus Auzenne, original act # 9853, Book Y-1, p. 40. On
October 3, 1870, Nezat sold Auzenne a tract of land two miles east of Opelousas on the road to Port Barre having one arpent front on the road with a
depth of six arpents for the price of $120.

Niles, Mrs. Edvina, to Alphonse Godeau and Zenon Rideau, original act
#8507, Book V-1, p. 158. On September 12, 1868, Mrs. Niles sold Godeau
and Rideau a fifty-acre tract of land on Dry Bayou for the price of $100.

Opelousas African Church to Joseph Simien, original act #11991, Book Z-1,
pp. 185–86. On February 15, 1871, the Opelousas African Church sold Joseph Simien a lot in Opelousas having fifty-two feet front on North Street
for the price of $350.

Paillet, Hilaire, and his wife acting on behalf of the Antoine Paillet Estate to Hilaire Louis Frilot, original act # 8166, Book U-1, p. 689. On January 13, 1868, Hilaire Paillet sold Hilaire Louis Frilot a 63.25-arpent tract of land for the price of $1,391.50.

Pitre, Caroline, and Jean Baptiste Rideau, *fils*, original act 11854, Book Z-1, p. 230. On March 14, 1872, Caroline Pitre and Jean Baptiste Rideau, *fils*, divided a tract of land in Prairie Plaisance having five arpents front by twenty-two arpents deep. Caroline, who was the mother of Louis Rideau, took the northern half of the property. [The implication of this document is that Louis Rideau died intestate and with no direct heirs. Therefore, his property went to his mother and his nephew.]

Pitre, Charles, estate of, to Jean Baptiste Rideau, estate auction, Book V-1, p. 31. On March 27, 1867, Jean Baptiste Rideau entered the high bid of $450 on a 42.33-acre tract of land in the Charles Pitre succession. The land was located in Grand Bois.

Pitre, Marie Melanie, widow of Joachim Pitre, to François Rideau, original act # 9483, Book X-1, p. 349. On February 14, 1870, Marie Pitre sold François Rideau a tract of land containing thirty-five arpents for the price of $175.90. This was land Joachim Pitre had sold to Joseph Lucien Perrodin but to which he held the mortgage. When Pitre died, Perrodin, unable to pay the mortgage, restored to his estate the land, which the widow then sold to Rideau.

Prudhomme, Louis, to Olympie Donato, original act #12056, Book Z-1, p. 366. On June 29, 1872, Prudhomme sold Donato a fractional town lot in Opelousas for the price of $25. The lot contained forty-six one-hundredth of an arpent, fronted on North Street and adjoined the land already owned by Olympie Donato.

Rideau, Jean Baptiste, to Preval Rideau and Mandeville Bowling and Graylor, original act #26698, Book T-2, p. 319. On October 7, 1886, Jean Baptiste transferred title to a 120-acre tract of land to Preval Rideau and Mandeville Bowling and Graylor. The property transferred was lot #1 of the estate of Zenon Rideau and had been acquired by Jean Baptiste in the partition of the estate on June 2, 1882. He owed money to Preval and to Mandeville Bowling, and Graylor and had not paid anything.

Rideau, Preval, to Samuel Knowlton and Company, original act # 26987, Book T-2, p. 593. On December 1, 1886, Preval sold Knowlton a four-acre tract of land at Goshen Station on the Texas and Pacific Railroad. The property, described as having 1,313 feet front along the tracks, sold for the price of $800. This is the original town site for the town of Palmetto.

Rideau, Zenon, to Jean Baptiste Soileau, *fils*, original act # 5346, Book T-1,

p. 252. On April 25, 1861, Rideau sold Soileau a Negro slave named Charlot, twenty-seven years of age, for the price of $2,200. The terms of the sale were that Soileau would make three equal payments at 8 percent interest on April 1, 1862, April 1, 1863, and April 1, 1864. In the document Zenon acknowledges owing Preval, aged twenty, and Eugenie, aged fifteen, each $100 from the succession of his deceased wife, Heloise Lavigne. [Soileau subsequently defaulted in his payments and Zenon Rideau brought suit in St. Landry District Court, September 27, 1866. Soileau refused to pay because he had not received full benefit of the transaction since the slave had been freed by military action and the Thirteenth Amendment. The court dismissed the suit. St. Landry Parish Civil District Court Suit 10058.]

Rideau, Zenon, to Marcelin Julien, a resident of Old Grand Prairie, original act #12251, Book Z-1, p. 513. On September 23, 1872, Zenon Rideau sold Julien a twenty-arpent plantation in Faubourg near Grand Prairie for the price of $150.

Rideau, Zenon, to Yacinthe Lafleur and Lucy Lafleur and their children, Marie Madeline, Joseph, Colombo, and Christoval, also Mary and Jules Rideau, orphans, original act #9233, Book X-1, p. 195. On September 16, 1869, Zenon made a donation to the above-named individuals of a plantation containing 166 acres on Bayou Petite Prairie which he had acquired from George Moss. He also donated to them his branding iron with twenty-five head of gentle cattle. He made some specific reservations:

1. The property was to remain in the possession of the donor and in community, after he died, until the youngest named reached the age of twenty-one.

2. Preval Rideau was to manage the property and be the guardian of the minor children.

3. After the youngest reached the age of twenty-one, and if the donor was deceased, the property was to be equally divided between all surviving members named in the donation.

Roberie, Marius, to Vilner Rideau and Thomas Duncan, original Act # 9196, Book X-1, pp. 125–26. On November 27, 1869, Roberie sold Rideau and Duncan a 120-arpent tract of land in Grand Prairie for the price of $600.

Sheriff and David Saizan to Antoine Alphonse Meuillon, sheriff's sale, Book U-1, p. 225. On July 7, 1866, the sheriff seized and sold the property of David Saizon in the case of Meuillon v. Saizon. Meuillon held a mortgage on a two-hundred-arpent tract of land with nine arpents front on the north side of Bayou Teche running in depth on the public road leading from Auzenne's Bridge and Port Barre. Meuillon bid $1,900, the amount of his mortgage. Meuillon had originally acquired the land from the Joseph Andrus estate.

Simien, Marie, estate of, to heirs of Marie Simien, partition, original act #13587, Book B-2, p. 584. Valentin Ledet took twenty-five arpents, Antoine Ledet took twenty-five arpents, Marie Ledet took twenty-five arpents, and Louis Simien, the surviving spouse and tutor to his minor children, Louis and Marie, took for his children twenty-five arpents.

Simien, François, to Adele Provost, wife of Baptiste F. Simien, donation, original act #12301, Book Z-1, p. 548. On November 12, 1872, François gave his daughter-in-law a forty-acre tract in Bois Mallet. This was the same land he purchased the same day from Etienne LeJeune, *fils*.

Simien, George, *père*, estate of, to Joseph Sublice and Pierre Derbanne, public auction, George Simien, *fils*, administrator, Book V-1, p. 315. On March 15, 1869, George Simien held a public auction to sell two tracts of land in Bois Mallet belonging to the estate of his father. Joseph Sublice purchased a thirty-acre tract for the high bid of $262.50. Pierre Derbanne purchased an eighteen-acre tract for $48.

Thierry, Alexander, *père*, estate of, to Alexander Thierry *fils*, public auction, Book V-1, p. 31. On March 27, 1868, Thierry, *fils*, entered the high bid of $440 for a two-and-one-half-arpent front on Bayou Grand Louis and forty-arpent depth tract of land in the quartier Plaisance.

Thompson, Clarissa, widow of Levi Thompson, to Zenon Rideau, original act #11861, Book Z-1, p. 234. On February 13, 1872, Zenon Rideau purchased from Clarissa Thompson, an eighty-acre tract immediately to the east of the tract he already owned on Bayou Petite Prairie for the price of $550. [The index identified this document as Clarissa, widow of Jacob Anselm, to Zenon Rideau; the document contained the information listed above.]

Vasseur, Jean, to Jean Baptiste Rideau, who lived near Pointe Meuillon, original act # 7736, Book U-1, p. 464. On February 18, 1867, Vasseur sold Rideau a twenty-arpent tract in Prairie Plaisance bordered by Coulee Bataille for the price of $230. The terms of the conveyance indicate that Rideau paid $100 in U.S. bills, $100 in gold, and signed a note for $30.

Additional Unabstracted Conveyances
Involving Members of the Same Nine Creole of Color Families
Compiled by Claude F. Oubre and Keith P. Fontenot

Andrus, C. B., to Eliza Lemelle, original Act #15786, Conveyance Book E-2, p. 413. On December 17, 1877, Andrus sold to Lemelle a five-acre tract located between Opelousas and Washington for the price of $80.

Andrus, C. B., to Pableau Donato, original act #15766, Conveyance Book E-2, p. 398. On December 3, 1877, Andrus sold to Donato a five-acre tract located near Opelousas on Hill Bayou for the price of $100.

Aubespin, A., to Elbert Gantt, original act #15010, Conveyance Book D-2, p. 529. On December 11, 1876, Aubespin sold to Gantt a town lot in Washington (twenty-five acres) for the price of $800.

Aubespin, Malveau, et al, to D. Lalanne, sheriff's sale, Conveyance Book E-2, p. 243. On July 7, 1877, Lalanne entered the high bid of $760 on a town lot in the town of Washington at the sheriff's sale.

Aubespin, Ozenne, to A. Aubespin, original act #14140, Conveyance Book C-2, p. 348. On October 9, 1875, Ozenne Aubespin sold to A. Aubespin a town lot in Washington for the price of $800.

Auzenne, Euzebe, to Simeon Birotte, original act #16740, Conveyance Book F-2, p. 635. On March 10, 1870, Auzenne sold to Birotte a town lot in Washington for the price of $600.

Auzenne, Philogene, to Pierre E. Frilot, Original act #16882, Conveyance Book G-2, p. 108. On May 22, 1879, Auzenne sold to Frilot two separate tracts, containing sixty superficial arpents each, located in Prairie Plaisance for the price of $400.

Baillo, Kenneth, to Cornelius Donato, original act #16308, Conveyance Book F-2, p. 202. On September 25, 1878, Baillo sold to Donato two separate tracts of land. The first, located three miles west of Opelousas, contained 255 acres, while the second, located in the big woods, contained 50 acres. The two tracts together sold for a total price of $1,200.

Bell, William G., to Adelaide Frilot, original act #15878, Conveyance Book E-2, p. 493. On January 12, 1878, Bell sold to Miss Frilot a town lot in Opelousas on Bellevue Street for the price of $600.

Bernard, Martin, to Zepherin Lemelle, original act #15696, Conveyance Book E-2, p. 337. On October 31, 1877, Bernard sold to Lemelle a fifty-acre tract in Prairie Laurent for the price of $150. The tract is further described as being lot 24 in Section 53, Township 7 South, Range 4 East.

Castein, J. A., to Patsy Lemelle, original act #13511, Conveyance Book B-2, p. 501. On October 3, 1874, Castein sold to Lemelle four town lots in Opelousas for the price of $150. The lots are described as being bounded by Franklin, Walnut, Union, and Madison streets.

Clunier, Eloise, to Estelle Auzenne, wife of Agenor Giron, original act #14833, Conveyance Book D-2, p. 271. On August 16, 1876, Clunier sold to Auzenne a twenty-two-arpent tract located three-fourths of a mile south of the courthouse in Opelousas for the price of $264.

Cooke, Mrs. Mary Nix, to Joachime Miron, wife of Adolphe Donato, original act #15443, Conveyance Book E-2, p. 107. On May 14, 1876, Cooke sold to Mrs. Donato a town lot containing 1.29 acres and located in the town of Opelousas, for the price of $60.

Dejean, Anais, to Jean Baptiste Lemelle, original act #14413, Conveyance Book

C-2, p. 634. On February 2, 1876, Dejean sold to Lemelle a forty-arpent tract on Bayou Teche for the price of $250.

Derbonne, Freedman, to Wilfred Simien, original act #18088, Conveyance Book G-2, p. 380. On November 17, 1879, Derbonne sold to Simien a twenty-five-arpent tract in Mallet for the price of $100.

Donato, Auguste, *fils,* to François A. Donato, Conveyance Book A-2, p. 457. On September 25, 1873, Auguste sold to François a five- by fifty-four-arpent tract located on Bayou Teche for the price of $2,000.

Donato, Auguste, to Pauline Dorsey, wife of Gerard Donato, and Rufus Bruxton, original act #12713, Conveyance Book A-2, p. 218. On January 15, 1873, Donato sold to Dorsey and Bruxton a ten-arpent tract of land located east of and near the town of Opelousas for the price of $650.

Donato, B. A., et al., to Mrs. Louis Frilot, original act #14770, Conveyance Book D-2, p. 215. On July 10, 1876, Donato sold to Mrs Frilot three lots in the town of Opelousas for the price of $79.20.

Donato, Clarissa, estate of, to Gustave Donato, Conveyance Book A-2, p. 591. On November 26, 1873, Gustave Donato bought several town lots in Opelousas from the estate for the price of $1,500.

Donato, Clarissa, estate of, to François Alcide Donato, Conveyance Book A-2, p. 439. On September 5, 1873, François Alcide Donato purchased a town lot in Washington from the estate for the price of $1,400.

Donato, Cornelius, to Henry L. Garland, original act #16761, Conveyance Book G-2, p. 6. On March 19, 1879, Donato sold to Garland a fifty-arpent tract of woodland near Plaisance for the price of $150. The tract is further described as being lot 2 of section 74, Township 5 South, Range 3 East.

Donato, François A., to Augustave Lazare, original act #13736, Conveyance Book B-2, p. 748. On January 4, 1875, Donato sold to Lazare a two-and-one-half-arpent by fifty-four-arpent tract on Bayou Teche for the price of $1,000.

Donato, François A., to Sevant Williams, original act #13735, Conveyance Book B-2, p. 747. On January 4, 1875, Donato sold to Williams a two-and-one-half-arpent by fifty-four-arpent tract on Bayou Teche for the price of $1,000.

Donato, Hilaire, to Narcisse Donato, original act #12861, Conveyance Book A-2, p. 382. On July 28, 1873, Hilaire sold to Narcisse a thirty-six-acre tract on Bayou Canne for the price of $100. The tract is further described as being the southeast quarter of section 38, Township 9 South, Range 2 West.

Donato, Jean-Baptiste, to David Roos, original act #19711, Conveyance Book I-2, p. 552. On May 7, 1881, Donato sold to Roos a fifty-acre tract located two miles east of Opelousas for the price of $262.

Donato, Julie, estate of, to Eugenie Donato, widow of Leon Manse, Conveyance Book C-2, p. 795. On April 11, 1876, Eugenie Donato purchased from the estate some town lots in Opelousas for the price of $1,000.

Donato, Marie Louise, to Joseph Pasquier, original act #13713, Conveyance Book B-2, p. 728. On December 30, 1874, Donato sold to Pasquier a town lot in Opelousas for the price of $1,500.

Donato, Marianne, widow of Rigobert Lemelle, to Catherine Frilot, wife of Homer Fuselier, original act #18371, Conveyance Book G-2, p. 677. On February 6, 1880, Donato sold to Frilot a three- by seven-arpent tract in Church Prairie for the price of $168.

Doucet, François, to Treville Rideau, original act # 8171, Conveyance Book U-1, p. 692. On December 28, 1867, Doucet sold to Rideau a four- by thirteen-arpent tract in Plaisance for the price of $400.

Dubuison, Edward, and Theodule Fontenot, to Ozenne Aubespin, original act #14137, Conveyance Book C-2, p. 345. On October 8, 1875, Dubuison and Fontenot sold to Aubespin a town lot in Washington for the price of $1,000.

Duson, C. C., Sheriff, to Marie Louise Lemelle, wife of Joseph D. Lemelle, Conveyance Book G-2, p. 510. On January 2, 1880, Marie Louise Lemelle purchased a town lot in Opelousas at a sheriff's sale for the price of $40. The property seized and sold by the sheriff was that of Austin Lacomb.

Estorge, Dame Marie Cora, widow of Bernard I. Salles, to Catherine Frilot, original act #13140 Conveyance Book B-2, p. 106. On January 3, 1874, Dame Estorge sold a town lot in Opelousas to Catherine Frilot for the price of $250.

Frilot, Anne Paillet, veuve of Louis C. Frilot, to Cora Estorge Sales, original act #1278, Conveyance Book A-2, p. 213. On March 31, 1873, Frilot sold to Sales a town lot in Opelousas for the price of $1,000.

Frilot, Adelaide, to Fannie E. McKinny, original act #15911, Conveyance Book E-2, p. 527. On January 22, 1878, Frilot sold to McKinny a town lot in Opelousas for the price of $600.

Frilot, Catherine, wife of Homer Fuselier, to David Roos, original act #19344, Conveyance Book I-2, p. 189. On January 27, 1881, Frilot sold to Roos a three- by seven-arpent tract of prairie land located two and one-half miles north of Opelousas for the price of $168.

Frilot, Hilaire L., and wife, to Catherine L. Goodloe, original act #16575, Conveyance Book F-2, p. 495. On January 30, 1879, Frilot sold to Goodloe a town lot in Opelousas for the price of $800.

Frilot, Hilaire L., and wife, to Mrs. H. T. Goodloe, wife of Henry T. Goodloe, original act #15934, Conveyance Book E-2, p. 537. On July 23, 1878, Frilot sold to Goodloe a sixty-three-acre tract for the price of $800. Although no location is given, the adjacent property owners were on the north, Sittig and

Hilaire Paillet; on the south, James Houston; on the east, B. A. Donato; and west Agenor Giron.

Frilot, L. Hilaire, to Charles Edward Lemelle, original act #14118, Conveyance Book C-2, p. 319. On September 10, 1875, Frilot sold to Lemelle two town lots in Opelousas for the price of $2,200.

Garland, Henry L., agent of Céleste Garland, to Hilaire L. Frilot, original act #15846, Conveyance Book E-2, p. 463. On December 27, 1877, Garland sold to Frilot forty-five arpents of prairie land one mile north of Opelousas on the road leading to Ville Platte for the price of $682.

Garland, Henry L., agent of Céleste Garland, to François A. Donato, original act #14960, Conveyance Book D-2, p. 404. On November 22, 1876, Garland sold to Donato a fifty-arpent tract of land two miles north of Opelousas for the price of $750.

Garland, Henry L., agent of Céleste Garland, to François A. Donato, original act #15456, Conveyance Book E-2, p. 120. On May 19, 1877, Garland sold to Donato a twenty-four-arpent tract of land (no location given but if it was Céleste's land it was north of Opelousas) for the price of $360.

Giron, Henry, to Emma Auzenne, wife of Alcide Frilot, and Eusèbe Auzenne, original act #13740, Conveyance Book B-2, p. 752. On January 4, 1875, Giron sold to the Auzennes a town lot in Washington for the price of $2,000.

Goudchaux, L., to Zenon Rideau, original act #18385, Conveyance Book G-2, p. 693. On February 3, 1880, Goudchaux sold to Rideau a forty-four-acre tract of land on Dry Bayou for the price of $450.

Hetherwick, John R., et al., to Adelaide Frilot, original act #13768, Conveyance Book B-2, p. 774. On January 15, 1875, Hetherwick sold to Frilot a town lot in Opelousas for the price of $600.

Joubert, Sophie, widow of François P. Pitre, Sr., to Valsin and Alfred Simien, original act #15174, Conveyance Book D-2, p. 631. On October 31, 1872, Joubert sold to the Simiens a fifty-arpent tract for the price of $200. The transaction was not recorded until January 19, 1877.

Lastrapes, Céleste Garland, through her agent Henry L. Garland, to Thérèse Martin Semien, original act #12540, Conveyance Book A-2, p. 69. On February 7, 1873, Garland sold to Semien a town lot in Washington for the price of $600.

Lastrapes, Victor, to Evelina Lemelle, his wife, original act #14336, Conveyance Book C-2, p. 549. On January 11, 1876, Lastrapes sold to his wife a town lot in Opelousas for the price of $900.

Ledé, Antoine, et al., to Clementine Provost, original act #19220, Conveyance Book I-2, p. 72. On December 11, 1880, Ledé sold to Provost thirty-two arpents of prairie land for the price of $92.

Ledé, Antoine, et al., to Olive Simien, original act #19219, Conveyance Book I-2, p. 71. On December 11, 1880, Ledé sold to Olive Simien a twenty-five-arpent tract in Prairie Mallet for the price of $75.

Ledé, Antoine, her husband, to Celestine Simien, his wife, original act #12214, Conveyance Book Z-1, p. 485. On October 4, 1872, Ledé, in a document designated as a *dation en paiement,* conveyed to his wife a twenty-five-arpent tract valued at $275 and some livestock valued at $509.

Lemelle, Charles E., to Rosina Prather, wife of Pierre Titard, original act #15518, Conveyance Book E-2, p. 182. On July 5, 1877, Lemelle sold to Prather a town lot in Opelousas for the price of $780.

Lemelle, Charles E., to Hilaire L. Frilot, original act #13476, Conveyance Book B-2, p. 458. Lemelle sold to Frilot two town lots in Opelousas for the price of $2,200.

Lemelle, Charles E., to Joseph M Hayes, original act #16137, Conveyance Book F-2, p. 14. On March 28, 1878, Lemelle sold to Hayes a town lot in Opelousas for the price of $600.

Lemelle, estate of Rigobert, to Marianne Lemelle, widow of Rigobert Lemelle, Conveyance Book G-2, pp. 454–56. On December 4, 1879, the estate sold to Marianne Lemelle a four- by eight-arpent tract one and one-half miles north of Opelousas for the price of $1,000.

Lemelle, François and wife, estate of, to Leon Lemelle, Rigobert Lemelle, and the widow of Charles Lemelle, original act #16649, Conveyance Book F-2, p. 558. The estate sold to Leon, Rigobert, and Charles's widow a four- by eighty-arpent tract for the price of $2,010.

Lemelle, Leon, and Euphemie Lemelle, to Marianne Lemelle, original act #18182, Conveyance Book G-2, p. 491. On December 18, 1878, the Lemelles partitioned a 4- by 80 or 320-arpent tract of land one and one-half miles north of Opelousas.

Lemelle, Leon, *veuve,* partition with Charles and Rigobert Lemelle and the widow of Charles Lemelle, original act #16705, Conveyance Book F-2, p. 601. On March 1, 1878, the Lemelles partitioned a 320-arpent tract near Opelousas.

Lemelle, Leontine, wife of Hilaire L. Frilot, to Helena Brown, widow of Hippolyte Martin, original act #16794, Conveyance Book G-2, p. 26. On April 9, 1879, Lemelle sold to Brown a town lot in Opelousas for the price of $150.

Lemelle, Marie L, wife of Joseph D. Donato, to Charles Lemelle, original act #12799, Conveyance Book A-2, p. 305. On June 9, 1873, Marie Lemelle sold to Charles Lemelle a town lot in Opelousas for the price of $100.

Lemelle, Marie Louise, wife of Joseph D. Donato, to Alfred Joseph Esterling, original act #15659, Conveyance Book E-2, p.308. On October 1, 1877,

Lemelle sold Esterling a sixty-two-arpent tract southwest of Opelousas for the price of $1,540.

Meuillon, Celestine A., estate of, through Pierre Frilot, the natural tutor of the heirs, to Philogene Auzenne, Conveyance Book G-2. p. 109. On May 30, 1879, acting for the heirs, Frilot sold to Auzenne a fifty-arpent tract of woodland on Bayou Teche in Prairie Laurent for the price of $400.

Meuillon, Clementine, wife of Philogene Ozenne, and Leocadie Meuillon, wife of Jules Frilot, exchange, original act #16834, Conveyance Book G-2, p. 66. On April 14, 1879, the Meuillon sisters exchanged two tracts of land; one is described as being twenty arpents on Bayou Teche in Prairie Laurent and the other is described as containing one-and-one-fourth by sixteen arpents in Prairie Laurent along a ditch called Fossé Plat.

Meuillon, Marie, and Josephine Lasassier, partition, original act #19697, Conveyance Book I-2, p. 540. On May 2, 1881, Meuillon and Lasassier partitioned a five- by fifty-four-arpent tract on Bayou Teche in Prairie Laurent.

Ortego, Jean Baptiste, to Jean Rideau and James and Harry Foreman, Original act #10065, Conveyance Book Y-1, p. 220. On January 21, 1871, Ortego sold to Rideau and the Foremans two tracts of land in the Ville Platte prairie, one was fifty-two and one-half arpents and the second was ten arpents of woodland. The total price for the two tracts was $650.

Perrodin, Auguste, et al., to Celestine Simien, wife of Antoine Lede, original act #16684, Conveyance Book F-2, p. 582. On February 19, 1879, the firm of J. and A. Perrodin sold to Simien a twenty-five-arpent tract in Mallet for $50.

Perrodin, Auguste, to Jean Baptiste Rideau, original act #18707, Conveyance Book H-2, pp. 119–30. On May 19, 1880, the firm of J. and A. Perrodin sold to Rideau a tract of land described as having 348 feet on the public road leading from Opelousas to Ville Platte, at Garrigues Bridge for the price of $100.

Perrodin, Jules and Auguste, to Charles E. Lemelle, original act #15678, Conveyance Book E-2, p. 325. On October 22, 1877, the firm of Jules and Auguste Perrodin sold to Charles Lemelle a sixty-two-acre tract for the price of $641.

Pitre, François L., to Marcelin Simien and Céleste Prevost, original act # 7830, Conveyance Book U-1, p. 511. On April 16, 1867, Pitre sold to Simien and Prevost the southwest one-quarter of section 7, Township 6 South, Range 3 East, at Mallet for the price of $400.

Pitre, Melanie Josette Pierre, to François Rideau, original act #16090, Conveyance Book E-2, p. 690. On April 12, 1878, Pitre sold to Rideau a fifteen-arpent tract in Plaisance for the price of $90.

Rideau, François, to Martin DeRosier, original act #16436, Conveyance Book

F-2, p. 367. On December 5, 1878, Rideau sold to DeRosier a twenty-five-arpent tract at Plaisance for the price of $500.

Rideau, Jean Baptiste, to Celestine and Eulalie Gallot, wife of Narcisse Lavigne, et al., original act #16145, Conveyance Book F-2, p. 12. On April 9, 1878, Rideau sold to the Gallots a fifty-arpent tract at Plaisance, a twenty-five-arpent tract in Prairie Ronde, and an ox cart for the price of $1,500.

Rideau, Jean Baptiste, and Jean Golbert Rideau, exchange, original act #16102, Conveyance Book E-2, p. 698. On April 9, 1878, the Rideaus exchanged four tracts of land: the first contained forty-five arpents, the second contained forty-two arpents, the third contained forty-two arpents, and the fourth contained fifty arpents. The only tract with a location given is the fifty-arpent tract in Plaisance.

Rideau, Jean Baptiste, to J. Bolbere Rideau, original act #14667, Conveyance Book D-2, p. 47. On May 1, 1876, Jean Baptiste Rideau sold to J. Bolbere Rideau a 233-acre tract in Plaisance for the price of $3,000.

Rideau, Jean Baptiste, to Mary Ann Duchesne, original act #14701, Conveyance Book D-2, p. 118. On May 18, 1876, Rideau sold to Duchesne a twenty-five-arpent tract in Plaisance for $300.

Rideau, Jean Baptiste, to Carl Wolff, original act #16798, Conveyance Book G-2, p. 29. On April 14, 1879, Rideau sold to Wolff two tracts of land. The first contained 94 acres on Bayou Petit Prairie, and the second contained 180 acres at Bayou Negrofoot or Tupper Flat. The sale price for both tracts was $379.

Rideau, Jean Baptiste, to New Orleans and Pacific Rail Road Co. Right of Way, original act #19140, Conveyance Book I-2, p. 5. On September 13, 1877, Rideau conveyed to the railroad company a 150-wide right-of-way. No specific location is mentioned in the conveyance.

Rideau, Jean Bolbert, to Jean Baptiste Rideau, original act #18536, Conveyance Book H-2, p. 101. On March 29, 1880, Jean Golbert Rideau sold to Jean Baptiste Rideau four tracts of land for a total price of $5,816. The tracts were mostly in Plaisance and contained 183 arpents, 45 arpents, 42.3 arpents and 42.3 arpents, respectively.

Rideau, Louis, et al., to Jean René Bellaire Fontenot and Octave P. Vidrine, original act #19283, Conveyance Book I-2, p. 127. On December 10, 1880, Rideau sold to Fontenot and Vidrine a fifty-arpent tract at Belaire Cove for the price of $160.

Rideau, Preval, to New Orleans and Pacific Railroad Co., Right of Way, original act #19146, Conveyance Book I-2, p. 9. On September 13, 1877, Rideau conveyed to the railroad company a 150-foot right-of-way. No specific location is indicated in the conveyance.

Rideau, Armentine Buvin, widow of Julien C. Rideau, to Lucien Perrodin, original act # 9893, Conveyance Book Y-1, p. 66. On September 15, 1876, Rideau sold to Perrodin a two-arpent tract of land in Plaisance for the price of $30.

Rideau, Zenon, to Arnaud Ramare, original act #19466, Conveyance Book I-2, p. 287. On January 27, 1881, Rideau sold to Ramare a forty-four-acre tract for the price of $600.

Rideau, Zenon, to Hilaire Daniel, original act #17071, Conveyance Book G-2, p. 273. On September 10, 1879, Rideau sold to Daniel a 120-acre tract on Bayou Petit Prairie for the price of $2,000.

Rideau, Zenon, to Marianne Capitain, original act # 6809, Conveyance Book T-1, p. 703. On December 8, 1865, Rideau sold to Capitain a two-hundred-arpent tract at Faubourg of old Grand Prairie for the price of $900.

Rideau, Zenon, to New Orleans and Pacific Railroad Co., right-of-way, original act #19147, Conveyance Book I-2, p. 10. On September 13, 1877, Rideau conveyed a 150-foot right-of-way to the railroad company.

Rideau, Zenon, to Odum Guillory, original act #19454, Conveyance Book I-2, p. 276. On January 27, 1881, Rideau sold to Guillory a forty-acre tract on Bayou Petite Prairie for the price of $350.

Saunier, Carlos, to Eugenie Donato, original act # 14235, Conveyance Book C-2, p. 447. On November 26, 1875, Saunier sold to Donato two tracts of land and some livestock for a total price of $381. The first tract was described as 100 arpents at Pointe aux Loups and the price was $100. The second tract was described as 220 arpents at Mallet and the price was $150. The livestock sold for $131.

Schmidt, J. B., of Eulalie Lemelle, original act #13916, Conveyance Book C-2, p. 122. On April 3, 1875, Lemelle sold Schmidt a town lot in Washington for $600.

Semien, François, to Valery and Arcdius Godeau, original act #12755, Conveyance Book A-2, p. 258. On April 28, 1873, Semien sold the Godeaus a one-hundred-arpent tract of prairie land for the price of $500.

Semien, François, to Adele Provost, wife of Baptiste F. Simien, original act #12301, Conveyance Book Z-1, p. 548. On November 13, 1872, François donated a forty-arpent tract in the Mallet woods to Adelle Provost Simien.

Semien, Marie L., estate of, to Valcourt, Antoine, and Marie Ledet, original act #13587, Conveyance Book B-2, p. 584. On November 9, 1874, the heirs of Marie Semien partitioned a one-hundred-arpent tract among themselves.

Sheriff's sale to Francois A. Donato, Conveyance Book G-2, p. 345. On October 29, 1878, Francois Donato entered the high bid of $135 on a ten-arpent tract of land to the east of and near Opelousas. The land being auctioned off with that of Pauline Dorsey. [This transaction was not recorded until October 18, 1879.]

Simien, Francois, estate of, to Jules Perrodin, Conveyance Book D-2, p. 253. On August 15, 1876, Jules Perrodin purchased three tracts of land from the Francois Simien estate. The first tract was described as one hundred arpents of woodland for the price of $100. The second tract was described as being forty-five arpents for the price of $20, and the third tract was described as having fifty arpents for the price of $67. The total for all three tracts, located in Mallet, was therefore $187.

Simien, George, *fils,* to Marie Louise Simien, original act No 7752, Conveyance Book U-1, p. 488. On March 12, 1867, George Simien sold to Marie Louise Simien two tracts of land in the Mallet prairie for a total price of $100. The first tract was simply described as being fourteen arpents deep while the second tract was described as being seven by seven arpents.

Simien, George, *père,* estate of, to Josephine and Joseph Sullice, Conveyance Book V-1, p. 315. On March 14, 1865, the Simien estate sold to Josephine and Joseph Sullice two tracts of land in Mallet. The first tract, containing thirty acres, sold for $262, while the second tract, eighteen acres of woodland, sold for $48.

Smith, Leo, and wife, to Francois Rideau, original act #13557, Conveyance Book B-2, p. 546. On October 23, 1874, Smith sold to Rideau two tracts of land in Plaisance; one was twenty-five arpents of prairie land the other was twenty-five arpents of woodland. Rideau paid a total of $300 for both tracts.

Wartelle, Harry, and sisters, to Jean Baptiste Rideau, original act #16546, Conveyance Book F-2, p. 645. On January 4, 1879, Wartelle sold to Rideau a ninety-four-acre tract on Bayou Petite Prairie for the price of $705.

Wartelle, Harry, and sisters, to Zenon Rideau, original act #16545, Conveyance Book F-2, p. 464. On Janury 4, 1879, Wartelle sold to Zenon Rideau a thirty-acre tract on Bayou Petite Prairie for the price of $150.

PRIMARY SOURCES

Articles

Willey, Nathan. "Education of the Colored Population of Louisiana." *Harper's New Monthly Magazine* 33 (1866): 244–50.

Colonial Census Reports

Archivo General de Indias (AGI), Seville, Spain.
Census of Mulattoes and Free Negroes, [1770], Papeles Procedentes de Cuba (PPC), 188A, unpaginated.
Census of Opelousas, 1774, AGI, PPC, 189A, folios 106–10.

Federal Census Reports

1810 census, Louisiana schedules, Attakapas and Opelousas counties.
1820 census, Louisiana schedules, St. Landry, St. Martin, and St. Mary parishes.
1830 census, Louisiana schedules, Lafayette, St. Landry, St. Martin, and St. Mary parishes.
1840 census, Louisiana schedules, Calcasieu, Lafayette, St. Landry, St. Martin, and St. Mary parishes.
1850 census, Louisiana schedules, Calcasieu, Lafayette, St. Landry, St. Martin, St. Mary, and Vermilion parishes.
1860 census, Louisiana schedules, Calcasieu, Lafayette, St. Landry, St. Martin, St. Mary, and Vermilion parishes.
1870 census, Louisiana schedules, Calcasieu, Cameron, Iberia, Lafayette, St. Landry, St. Martin, St. Mary, and Vermilion parishes.
1880 census, Louisiana schedules, Calcasieu, Cameron, Iberia, Lafayette, St. Landry, St. Martin, St. Mary, and Vermilion parishes.
1940 census, Housing, Vol. 2, General Characteristics, U.S. Department of Commerce Report of the Census, 379.

Interviews

Interview of Mary Ellen Donato by Claude Oubre, 1971.
Interview of Irene Tenney, director of the Cajun and Creole Culture Center, by Carl A. Brasseaux, Berkeley, California, May 5, 1993.

Manuscripts

Archivo General de Indias, Seville, Spain.
  Papeles Procedentes de Cuba, legajos 188A, 188B, 189A.
Center for Louisiana Studies, University of Southwestern Louisiana, Lafayette, Louisiana.
  Juan Bautista Garic Papers, New Orleans Notarial Archives, microfilm copy in the Colonial Records Collection.
Louisiana State Archives and Records Service, Baton Rouge, Louisiana.
  Opelousas Colonial Records.
  Original Acts, St. Landry Parish Records.
Sabatier, George. Collection. Lafayette, Louisiana.
  Original Acts, Opelousas Post, 1786–93.
St. Landry Parish Clerk of Court's Office, St. Landry Parish Courthouse, Opelousas, Louisiana.
  Alienation Book 1.
  Civil District Suits, 1813–90.
  Colonial-era marriage records (microfilm copy), 1764–1805.
  Conveyance Books, 1805–90.
  Donation Book 2.
  Estate 81.
  Labyche Notarial Acts.
  Marriage Records, 1805–90.
  Microfile 017115.
  Miscellaneous Records, 1854–90.
  Mortgage Records, 1805–90.
  Notary Books A, AA, B.
  Partnership Book 2.
  Probate Court Records, 1805–90.
  Probates, 1805–90.
  Probate Court Suits, 1822–46.
  Recorder File 3142.
  Sheriff Book A.
  Tax Rolls, 1817–18.
St. Martin Parish Clerk of Court's Office, St. Martin Parish Courthouse, St.

Martinville, Louisiana (microfilm copies are also on deposit at the Center for Louisiana Studies, University of Southwestern Louisiana).
Original Acts, vols, 1–30.
Successions, numbers 1–225.

State Publications

Louisiana. *Acts of the Legislature, Vol. 1, Regular Session, 1970.* Baton Rouge: State of Louisiana, 1970.
————, Department of State. *Roster of Officials.* Baton Rouge: Louisiana Department of State, 1973–93.

Newspapers

Franklin Planters' Banner, 1870.
Lafayette Advertiser, 1869–90.
New Orleans Daily Picayune, 1859–60.
New Orleans States-Item, June 5–16, 1978.
Opelousas Courier, 1852–90.
Opelousas Journal, 1868–70.

Published Records and Abstracts

Barde, Alexandre. *Histoire des Comités de vigilance aux Attakapas.* [Hahnville, La.]: *Le Meschacébé,* 1861.
Conrad, Glenn R., comp. *St. Charles: Abstracts of the Civil Records of St. Charles Parish, 1700–1803.* Lafayette, La.: Center for Louisiana Studies, 1974.
Desdunes, Rodolphe Lucien. *A Few Words to Dr. DuBois "With Malice Toward None."* New Orleans: Desdunes, 1907.
————. *Our People and Our History.* Translated and edited by Sister Dorothea McCants. Baton Rouge: Louisiana State University Press, 1973.
Hébert, Donald J., comp. *Southwest Louisiana Records.* 39 vols. Cecilia, Eunice, and Rayne, La.: Hébert Publications, 1974–92.
Louisiana Reports Books, Martin Reports, N.S. Vol. 5. *Reports of the Louisiana Supreme Court Western Term, August and October 1826.*
Olmsted, Frederick Law. *The Slave States (Before the Civil War).* Edited with an introduction by Harvey Wish. New York: Capricorn Books, 1959.
U.S. House of Representatives. *Miscellaneous Document 211.* 42d Cong., 2d sess.
Vidrine, Jacqueline O., and Winston De Ville, comps. and eds. *Marriage Contracts of the Opelousas Post, 1766–1803.* [Ville Platte, La.]: Privately printed, 1960.

West's Louisiana Statutes. Revised Statutes, Sections 41:1 to 42:end. St. Paul, Minn.: West Publishing Co., 1990.

Woodson, Carter G., comp. *Free Negro Owners of Slaves in the United States in 1830, Together with Absentee Ownership of Slaves in the United States in 1830.* Washington, D.C.: Association for the Study of Negro Life and History, 1924.

Württemberg, Paul Wilhelm, Duke of. *Travels in North America, 1822–1824.* Translated by W. Robert Nitske. Edited by Savoie Lottinville. Norman: University of Oklahoma Press, 1973.

Articles

Foote, Ruth. "Zydeco Festival '90: The Creole Players Behind the Scenes." *Creole Magazine* 1 (December 1990): 18–19, 21.

SECONDARY SOURCES

Books

Ancelet, Barry Jean. *Cajun Music: Its Origins and Development.* Lafayette, La.: Center for Louisiana Studies, 1989.

Baker, Vaughan B., and Jean T. Kreamer, eds. *Louisiana Tapestry: The Ethnic Weave of St. Landry Parish.* Lafayette, La.: Center for Louisiana Studies, 1982.

Bergeron, Arthur W., Jr., and Jacqueline Olivier Vidrine. *Calendar of Documents of the Opelousas Post, 1764–1789.* Baton Rouge: Le Comité des Archives de la Louisiane, 1979.

Bethel, Elizabeth Rauh. *Promiseland: A Century of Life in a Negro Community.* Philadelphia: Temple University Press, 1981.

Brasseaux, Carl A. *Acadian to Cajun: Transformation of a People, 1803–1877.* Jackson: University Press of Mississippi, 1992.

———. *The Founding of New Acadia: The Beginnings of Acadian Life in Louisiana, 1765–1803.* Baton Rouge: Louisiana State University Press, 1987.

———. *Lafayette: Where Yesterday Meets Tomorrow, an Illustrated History.* Chatsworth, Calif.: Windsor Publications, 1990.

Brasseaux, Carl A., Glenn R. Conrad, and R. Warren Robison. *The Courthouses of Louisiana.* Lafayette, La.: Center for Louisiana Studies, 1977.

Burson, Caroline M. *The Stewardship of Don Esteban Miro, 1782–1792: A Study of Louisiana Based Largely on Documents in New Orleans.* New Orleans: American Printing Company, 1940.

Conrad, Glenn R. *Land Records of the Attakapas District,* Vol. 1, *Attakapas Domesday Book.* Lafayette, La.: Center for Louisiana Studies, 1990.

De Ville, Winston. *Opelousas: The History of a French and Spanish Military Post in America, 1716–1803.* Cottonport, La.: Polyanthos, 1973.

Dismukes, J. Philip. *The Center: A History of the Development of Lafayette, La.* Lafayette, La.: City of Lafayette, 1969.

Dominguez, Virginia Rosa. *White by Definition: Social Classification in Creole Louisiana.* New Brunswick, N.J.: Rutgers University Press, 1986.

Ficklen, John Rose. *History of Reconstruction in Louisiana.* Baltimore: Johns Hopkins Press, 1910.

Fischer, Roger A. *The Segregation Struggle in Louisiana, 1862–77.* Urbana: University of Illinois Press, 1974.

Gayarré, Charles Etienne Arthur. *History of Louisiana.* 4 vols. New Orleans: James A. Gresham, 1879.

Griffin, Harry Lewis. *Attakapas Country: A History of Lafayette Parish.* 1959; rpr. Gretna, La.: Pelican, 1974.

Hall, Gwendolyn Midlo. *Africans in Colonial Louisiana: The Development of an Afro-Creole Culture in the Eighteenth Century.* Baton Rouge: Louisiana State University Press, 1992.

Herrin, M. H. *The Creole Aristocracy: A Study of the Creoles of Southern Louisiana.* New York: Exposition Press, 1952.

Hirsch, Arnold R., and Joseph Logsdon, eds. *Creole New Orleans: Race and Americanization.* Baton Rouge: Louisiana State University Press, 1992.

MacDonald, Robert, John R. Kemp, and Edward F. Haas, eds. *Louisiana's Black Heritage.* New Orleans: Louisiana State Museum, 1979.

Meyers, Cheryl Bihm. *Palmetto: The Early Years (1803–1935).* Opelousas, La.: Privately printed, 1987.

Mills, Gary B. *The Forgotten People: Cane River's Creoles of Color.* Baton Rouge: Louisiana State University Press, 1977.

Olsen, Otto H. *The Thin Disguise: Turning Point in Negro History, Plessy v. Ferguson, a Documentary Presentation.* New York: Humanities Press, 1967.

Oubre, Claude F. *Forty Acres and a Mule: The Freedmen's Bureau and Black Land Ownership.* Baton Rouge: Louisiana State University Press, 1978.

Oukada, Larbi. *Louisiana French: An Annotated Linguistic Bibliography.* Lafayette, La.: Center for Louisiana Studies, 1979.

Roussève, Charles Barthélémy. *The Negro in Louisiana: Aspects of His History and His Literature.* New Orleans: Xavier University Press, 1937.

Sterkx, H. E. *The Free Negro in Ante-Bellum Louisiana.* Rutherford, N.J.: Fairleigh Dickinson University Press, 1972.

Vidrine, Jacqueline O., and Winston De Ville, comps. and eds. *Marriage Con-*

tracts of the Opelousas Post, 1766–1803. Ville Platte, La.: Privately printed, 1960.

Vincent, Charles. *Black Legislators in Louisiana during Reconstruction.* Baton Rouge: Louisiana State University Press, 1976.

Voorhies, Jacqueline K. *Some Late Eighteenth-Century Louisianians.* Lafayette, La.: Center for Louisiana Studies, 1973.

Woods, Frances Jerome. *Marginality and Identity: A Colored Creole Family Through Ten Generations.* Baton Rouge: Louisiana State University Press, 1972.

———. *Value Retention among Young Creoles.* Mellen Studies in Sociology, Vol. 5. Lewiston, N.Y.: Edwin Mellen Press, 1989.

Woodson, Carter G. *The Negro in Our History.* Washington, D.C.: Associated Publishers, 1927.

Articles

Allain, Mathé. "Slave Policies in French Louisiana." *Louisiana History* 21 (1980): 127–37.

Brasseaux, Carl A. "The Administration of Slave Regulations in French Louisiana, 1724–1766." *Louisiana History* 21 (1980): 139–58.

———. "Louisiana's Senegambian Legacy." In *Senegal: Peintures Narratives/ Narrative Paintings,* 52–60. Lafayette, La.: University Art Museum, University of Southwestern Louisiana, 1986.

——— "Opelousas and the Alabama Immigrants." *Attakapas Gazette* 14 (1979): 112–17.

——— "Prosperity and the Free Population of Lafayette Parish, 1850–1860." *Attakapas Gazette* 12 (1977): 105–8.

Brasseaux, Carl, and Mathé Allain. "Creoles." In *Report by Hamilton and Associates for Jean Lafitte National Park.* Opelousas, La.: Hamilton and Associates, 1987.

DeLatte, Carolyn E. "The St. Landry Riot: A Forgotten Incident of Reconstruction Violence." *Louisiana History* 17 (1976): 41–49.

Dunbar-Nelson, Alice. "People of Color in Louisiana." *Journal of Negro History* 2 (1917): 51–78.

Everett, Donald E. "Free Persons of Color in Colonial Louisiana." *Louisiana History* 7 (1966): 21–50.

Foner, Laura. "The Free People of Color in Louisiana and St. Domingue: A Comparative Portrait of Two Three-Caste Slave Societies." *Journal of Social History* 3 (1969–70): 406–30.

Hanger, Kimberly S. "Avenues to Freedom Open to New Orleans' Black Population, 1769–1779." *Louisiana History* 31 (1990): 237–64.

———. "Household and Community Structure among the Free Population of Spanish New Orleans, 1778." *Louisiana History* 30 (1989): 63–79.

Hardy, James D. "The Banality of Slavery." *Southern Studies* 25 (1986): 187–95.

Jones, Joseph H., and Vernon Parenton. "The People of Frilot Cove: A Study of Racial Hybrids." *American Journal of Sociology* 57 (1948): 145–49.

Oubre, Claude. "The Opelousas Riot of 1868." *Attakapas Gazette* 8 (1973): 139–51.

Reynolds, C. Russell. "Alfonso El Sabio's Laws Survive in the Civil Code of Louisiana." *Louisiana History* 12 (1971): 137–47.

Schafer, Judith K. "'Open and Notorious Concubinage': The Emancipation of Slave Mistresses by Will and the Supreme Court in Antebellum Louisiana." *Louisiana History* 27 (1987): 165–82.

Schweninger, Loren. "Antebellum Free Persons of Color in Postbellum Louisiana." *Louisiana History* 30 (1989): 345–64.

Stahl, Annie. "The Free Negro in Ante-bellum Louisiana." *Louisiana Historical Quarterly* 25 (1942): 301–96.

Tregle, Joseph G., Jr. "On That Word 'Creole' Again: A Note." *Louisiana History* 23 (1982): 193–98.

Theses and Dissertations

Dominguez, Virginia Rosa. "Behind the Semantic Curtain: Social Classification in Creole Louisiana." Ph.D. dissertation, Yale University, 1979.

Jones, Joseph H. "The People of Frilot Cove: A Study of a Racial Hybrid Community in Rural South Central Louisiana." M.A. thesis, Louisiana State University, 1950.

McTigue, Geraldine M. "Forms of Racial Interaction in Louisiana, 1860–1880." Ph.D. dissertation, Yale University, 1975.

Spitzer, Nicholas Randolph. "Zydeco and Mardi Gras: Creole Identity and Performance Genres in Rural French Louisiana." Ph.D. dissertation, University of Texas–Austin, 1986.

INDEX